TOP-NOTCH
KNITS

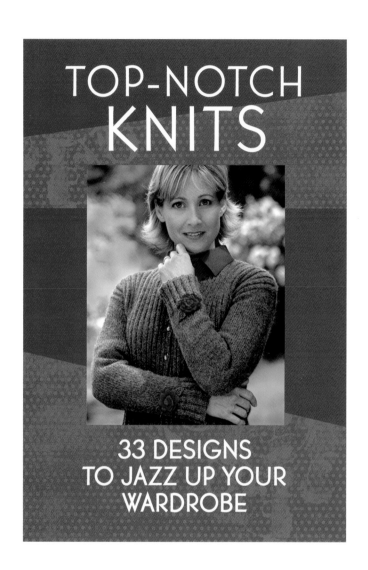

33 DESIGNS
TO JAZZ UP YOUR
WARDROBE

Martingale®
& C O M P A N Y

Top-Notch Knits: 33 Designs to Jazz Up Your Wardrobe
© 2009 by Martingale & Company

Martingale & Company®
20205 144th Ave. NE
Woodinville, WA 98072-8478 USA
www.martingale-pub.com

Printed in China
14 13 12 11 10 09   8 7 6 5 4 3 2 1

Library of Congress Cataloging-in-Publication Data is available upon request.

ISBN: 978-1-56477-942-7

The patterns in this book were previously published in one of the following books, all from Martingale & Company:

A Garden Stroll by Lori Ihnen
Basically Brilliant Knits by Melissa Matthay and Sheryl Thies
Everyday Style by Carol Rasmussen Noble
Knit It Now! by Julie Montanari
Knitted Shawls, Stoles, & Scarves by Nancie M. Wiseman
The Little Box of Knitted Ponchos and Wraps by Sandy Scoville
The Little Box of Sweaters by Melissa Matthay and Sheryl Thies
Perfectly Brilliant Knits by Melissa Matthay and Sheryl Thies
Style at Large by Carol Rasmussen Noble
Two Sticks and a String by Kerry Ferguson

credits

President & CEO • Tom Wierzbicki

Editor in Chief • Mary V. Green

Managing Editor • Tina Cook

Technical Editor • Ursula Reikes

Copy Editor • Marcy Heffernan

Design Director • Stan Green

Production Manager • Regina Girard

Illustrators • Laurel Strand & Robin Strobel

Cover & Text Designer • Shelly Garrison

Photographers • Brent Kane & John Hamel

mission statement

Dedicated to providing quality
products and service to inspire creativity.

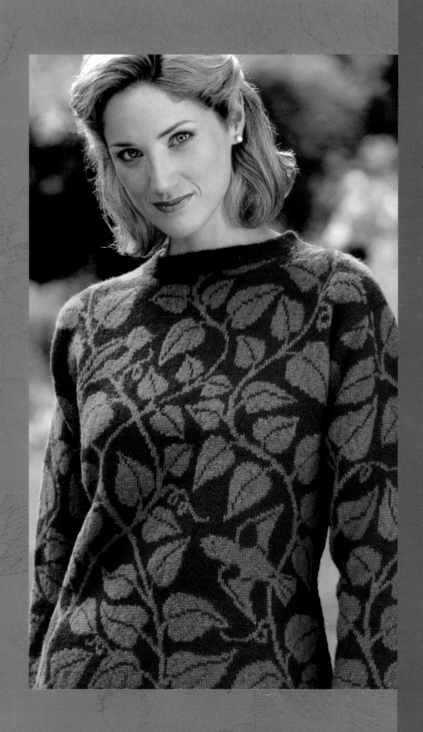

contents

introduction

Welcome to a great selection of gorgeous knits! You'll find inspiration on every page of this terrific knitwear collection from America's Best-Loved Knitting Books®. Packed with more than 30 projects, this volume features fabulous wearables from lacy scarves and wraps to summertime tanks and tees to cozy cardigans and pullovers.

Artistic scarves, shawls, and wraps. Now you can accent your wardrobe with stunning accessories in a variety of shapes and styles. Try the Garter Stitch Squares Scarf on page 11 and create easy-to-stitch mitered squares. Or wrap yourself in the delicate drape of a shawl, such as the Luxury in Cashmere Shawl on page 15 or the shimmery Circle-of-Elegance Shawl on page 17. If you're looking for a bit of lace knitting, try the Lavender Linen Lace Shawl on page 19 or the sumptuous tapered Lace Scarf on page 9.

Terrific tanks, tees, and shells. You won't have to fish for compliments when you wear the unique Shark Fin Tank on page 29! Detailed and eye-catching, this attractive piece includes crochet edges and a knit lace hem. For a slenderizing look, try the Braided Shell on page 31 and make artful use of a braided center cable.

You'll enjoy easy stitching and pastel colors as you create the Color-Block Shell on page 37. The youthful design is just the thing for wearing with a skirt or your favorite pair of jeans.

Pretty pullovers. This collection also features a generous assortment of pullovers in a wide range of styles, sizes, and yarns. The Cashmere-and-Silk Fitted Cowl on page 67 is specially designed to flatter fuller figures and includes instructions for sizes up to 3X.

To explore your passion for yarn, don't miss the Twisted-Yoke Pullover on page 61, which showcases a smooth silk-and-cashmere blend. If you have your eye on a lightweight yarn such as soft mohair, the Soft-Twist Tunic on page 55 is ideal.

Stylish cardigans and jackets. Want to make something truly warm and wonderful? Luxuriate in the rich textures of the Aran Cardigan on page 99 or the diagonal latticework of the Fake Cable Cardigan on page 115. For a lovely touch of romance, turn to the Rose Blossom Cardigan on page 95. The sleeves are embellished with three-dimensional red roses for the perfect finishing touch.

As you look through the captivating photos in this book, you'll find these and many other tempting projects. So pick some luxurious yarn, choose an exciting pattern, and create something you absolutely love!

SCARVES, SHAWLS, AND WRAPS

LACE SCARF

lace scarf

This sumptuous scarf starts at the middle with a provisional cast on and is knit from the center outward toward each tapered end.

By Nancie M. Wiseman

Skill Level: Intermediate ◖■■■▢

Finished Measurements: 7" x 70" after blocking

materials

A 450 yds of fingering-weight cashmere/silk blend ⓵

B 450 yds of fingering-weight kid mohair/silk blend ⓵

3 yards waste yarn for provisional cast on

Size 8 (5 mm) needles, or size required to obtain gauge

Crochet hook, size G/6 (4 mm)

gauge

18 sts and 24 rows = 4" in St st with 1 strand each of A and B held tog

directions

The scarf is worked from the center toward each end. Note that only right-side rows are charted. Work all wrong-side rows as: K5, purl to last 5 sts, K5.

Using 1 strand each of A and B held tog, CO 33 sts using provisional CO (see page 126). K5, P23, K5.

Work chart rows 1 through 16 once. Then work rows 17 through 30 a total of 9 times; for shorter or longer scarf, work fewer or more reps of rows 17 through 30 as desired. Work rem of chart through row 77.

Remove provisional CO, place sts on needle, and work second half of scarf as for first half.

finishing

Weave in all ends. Rinse out, roll in a towel, pin out, and lay flat to dry.

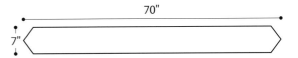

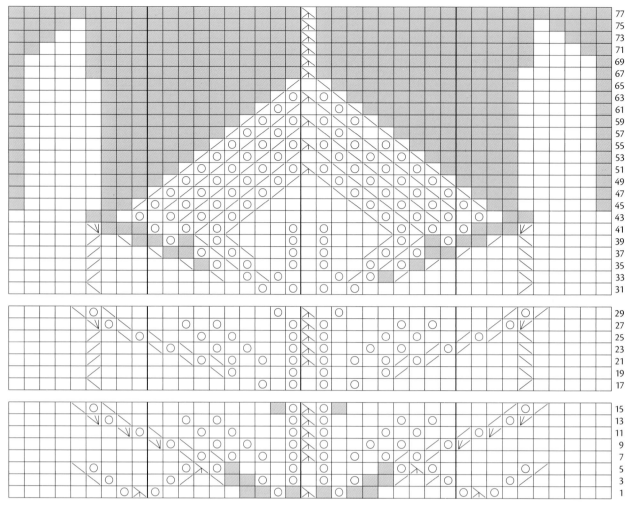

Key

☐	K
▨	No stitch
⊙	YO
◺	ssk
◹	K2tog
◲	CC dec (sl 2-K1-p2sso)
⩗	K3tog
◩	sl 1-K2tog-psso

All even-numbered (WS) rows: K5, purl to last 5 sts, K5.

For each half:
Work rows 1 through 16 once.
Work rows 17 through 30 a total of 9 times.
Work rem of chart through row 77.

garter stitch squares scarf

Mitered squares are worked in two sizes to create this colorful and easy-to-knit scarf.

By Nancie M. Wiseman

Skill Level: Intermediate ■■■◻

Finished Measurements: 8" x 61"

materials

A 300 yds of worsted-weight 100% wool (4)

B 300 yds of worsted-weight 100% wool (4)

Size 8 (5 mm) needles or size required to obtain gauge

gauge

One 21-stitch square = 2½"

patterns

SMALL SQUARE (Worked over 21 sts)

Row 1 and all odd rows: Knit.

Row 2: K9, sl 1-K2tog-psso, K9.

Row 4: K8, sl 1-K2tog-psso, K8.

Row 6: K7, sl 1-K2tog-psso, K7.

Row 8: K6, sl 1-K2tog-psso, K6.

Row 10: K5, sl 1-K2tog-psso, K5.

Row 12: K4, sl 1-K2tog-psso, K4.

Row 14: K3, sl 1-K2tog-psso, K3.

Row 16: K2, sl 1-K2tog-psso, K2.

Row 18: K1, sl 1-K2tog-psso, K1.

Row 20: Sl 1-K2tog-psso. Fasten off.

LARGE SQUARE (Worked over 41 sts)

Row 1 and all odd rows: Knit.

Row 2: K19, sl 1-K2tog-psso, K19.

Row 4: K18, sl 1-K2tog-psso, K18.

Row 6: K17, sl 1-K2tog-psso, K17.

Row 8: K16, sl 1-K2tog-psso, K16.

Row 10: K15, sl 1-K2tog-psso, K15.

Row 12: K14, sl 1-K2tog-psso, K14.

Row 14: K13, sl 1-K2tog-psso, K13.

Row 16: K12, sl 1-K2tog-psso, K12.

Row 18: K11, sl 1-K2tog-psso, K11.

Row 20: K10, sl 1-K2tog-psso, K10.

Row 22: K9, sl 1-K2tog-psso, K9.

Row 24: K8, sl 1-K2tog-psso, K8.

Row 26: K7, sl 1-K2tog-psso, K7.

Row 28: K6, sl 1-K2tog-psso, K6.

Row 30: K5, sl 1-K2tog-psso, K5.

Row 32: K4, sl 1-K2tog-psso, K4.

Row 34: K3, sl 1-K2tog-psso, K3.

Row 36: K2, sl 1-K2tog-psso, K2.

Row 38: K1, sl 1–K2tog–psso, K1.

Row 40: Sl 1–K2tog–psso. Fasten off.

directions

Use cable CO (see page 126) whenever casting on after picking up sts.

Following the diagram on facing page, proceed as follows:

Square 1: Using A, CO 21 sts. Work small square patt.

Square 2: Turn square 1 so diagonal line is to the left. Using B, PU 11 sts along left edge. CO 10 sts using cabled CO. Work small square.

Square 3: Using A, PU 11 sts along left edge of square 2. CO 10 sts using cabled CO. Work small square.

Square 4: Using B, PU 11 sts across top of square 3. CO 10 sts. Work small square.

Square 5: Using A, PU 11 sts across top of square 4. CO 10 sts. Work small square.

Square 6: Using B, PU 20 sts across top of squares 1 and 2, 1 st in the corner of square 3, 20 sts up edge of squares 4 and 5. Work large square.

Square 7: Using B, CO 11 sts. PU 10 sts across one half of top of square 6. Work small square.

Square 8: Using A, PU 10 sts down left side of square 7, 1 st in corner, 10 sts across rem half of square 6. Work small square.

Square 9: Using B, PU 10 sts down left side of square 8, 1 st in corner, 10 sts across top of square 5. Work small square.

Square 10: Using A, CO 11 sts. PU 10 sts across top of square 7. Work small square.

Square 11: Using B, CO 11 sts. PU 10 sts across top of square 10. Work small square.

Square 12: Using A, PU 20 sts down left side of squares 11 and 10, 1 st in corner and 20 more sts across top of squares 8 and 9. Work large square patt.

Squares 13–45: Rep squares 1 through 12 twice more, picking up sts instead of casting on sts for squares 1, 2, and 3. Work squares 1 through 9 once.

finishing

Side borders: On right-hand side of scarf and with RS of long edge facing you, using A, PU 10 sts on edges of small squares and 20 sts on edges of large squares. Knit 2 rows. BO loosely. Rep on long edge of left-hand side with B.

Bottom and top borders: On bottom edge and with RS facing you you, using A, PU 2 sts in side border, 10 sts across each small square, and 2 sts in side border. Knit 2 rows. BO loosely. Rep for top edge using B.

Weave in all ends. Steam gently if necessary.

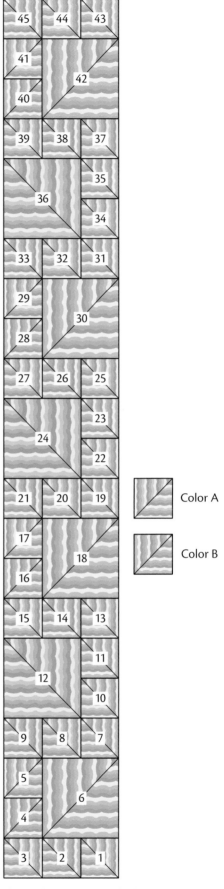

Color A

Color B

This diagram shows the order in which the squares are knit and the color used to knit them. Diagonal line shows the direction of decreases.

LUXURY IN CASHMERE SHAWL

luxury in cashmere shawl

Curl up on a rainy afternoon wrapped in this buttery-soft shawl, or wear it as the ultimate accessory over your finest dress or suit to add warmth and beauty.

By Sandy Scoville

Skill Level: Intermediate ◼◼◼▭

Finished Measurements: Approx 22" x 60" (without fringe)

materials

1140 yds of DK-weight 100% cashmere ③

Size 6 (4 mm) needles or size required to obtain gauge

Crochet hook, size E/4 (3.5 mm)

gauge

18 sts and 24 rows = 4" in St st

directions

CO 97 sts.

Row 1 (WS): P6, *(YO twice, K1) 5 times, P5, rep from * 8 times, end P1.

Row 2: K6, *(P1, drop YOs) 5 times, K5, rep from * 8 times, end K1.

Rows 3–8: Work rows 1 and 2 another 3 times.

Row 9: P1, (YO twice, K1) 5 times, *P5, (YO twice, K1) 5 times, rep from * 8 times, end P1.

Row 10: K1, (P1, drop YOs) 5 times, *K5, (P1, drop YOs) 5 times, rep from * 8 times, end K1.

Rows 11–16: Work rows 9 and 10 another 3 times.

Work rows 1–16 until shawl measures about 60", ending with completed row 8. BO all sts.

finishing

Fringe: Cut 194 strands, 24" long. Using crochet hook, attach 1 strand of fringe in each st along both short ends as follows: Fold fringe in half. Insert hook in stitch from back to front. Catch the folded fringe and pull it through the knitted piece, creating a loop. Draw the fringe ends through the loop and pull to tighten. Trim ends even.

Weave in ends. Steam gently if necessary.

Front view (above).
Back view (right).

CIRCLE-OF-ELEGANCE SHAWL

circle-of-elegance shawl

Wear this delicate shawl draped over your shoulders or as a dressy head covering. The soft drape of shimmery yarn will draw looks of approval.

By Sandy Scoville

Skill Level: Easy ◖▰▱▱▱◗

Finished Measurements: Approx 22" x 30"*

The shawl stretches, so the width will vary when worn.

materials

800 yds of worsted-weight rayon/nylon blend ribbon (4)

Size 8 (5 mm) circular needle (24") or size required to obtain gauge

1 stitch marker

gauge

20 sts and 24 rows = 4" in St st

directions

Normally when starting a project in the round, you need to be careful not to twist the cast-on stitches around the needle before joining them in a circle. In this project, you will deliberately twist the first few cast-on stitches around the needle. This is what creates the twist in the shawl.

Loosely CO 150 sts, pm, twist first few CO sts on LH needle around needle once and knit into first st in usual manner. Sl marker at beg of each rnd.

Rnd 1: Knit.

Rnd 2: Purl.

Rep rnds 1 and 2 until scarf measures about 22" from top to bottom when slightly stretched. BO sts loosely.

finishing

Weave in ends.

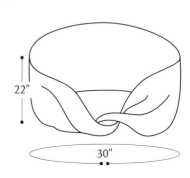

The diagram shows the full twist of the shawl. You can wear the shawl with the full twist in front, or arrange the shawl so that half of the twist is in front and the other half of the twist is in back, as shown in the photos (left).

LAVENDER LINEN LACE SHAWL

lavender linen lace shawl

Linen is a wonderful yarn for a summer shawl.
The crispness of the yarn gives a very distinct
look to the leaves.

By Nancie M. Wiseman

Skill Level: Intermediate ◼◼◼◻

Finished Measurements: Approx 61" x 28" after blocking

materials

650 yds of sport-weight 100% linen 【2】

Size 4 (3.5mm) circular needle (29"), or size required
to obtain gauge

gauge

20 sts and 28 rows = 4" in St st

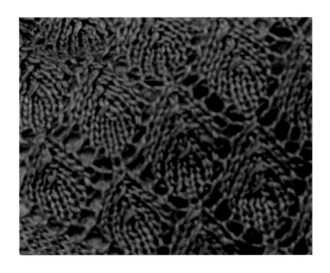

directions

Sl 1 st at beg of every row pw wyif.
This counts as 1 st on the chart.

CO 3 sts. Following chart on page 20, work rows 1
through 30 once. Work rows 31 through 46 a total
of 11 times, rep the 10-st center section as the shawl
enlarges. The charts for the edge sections will rem
the same throughout. The patt may be continued
if you desire a larger shawl. End with row 46. Knit 9
rows. BO loosely.

finishing

Weave in ends. Immerse shawl in cool water, rinse
out, and roll in a towel to absorb excess moisture.
Pin out on flat surface. Do not remove until dry.

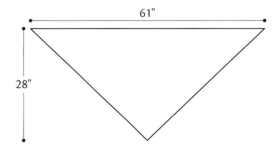

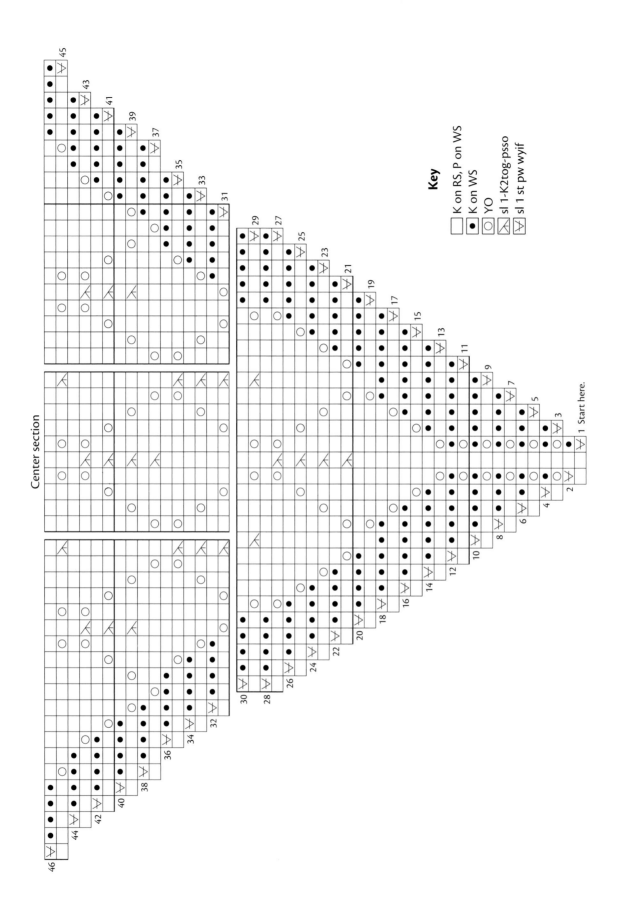

Key

		K on RS, P on WS
●		K on WS
○		YO
⊼		sl 1-K2tog-psso
⋏		sl 1 st pw wyif

Center section

Start here.

highland mist shawl

The traditional Shetland lace pattern called Crest o' the Wave is featured here in a handpainted lace-weight merino/silk blend. Blocking is important here; it's not until after it's blocked that the true beauty of the lace pattern is completely revealed.

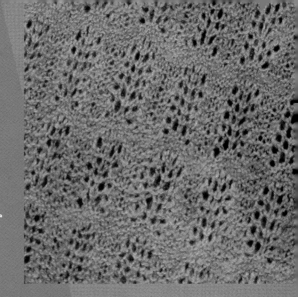

By Carol Rasmussen Noble

Skill Level: Easy ◖■□□

Finished Measurements: 16" x 60", plus 14" of fringe, after blocking

materials

1260 yards of lace-weight wool/silk blend 🔟

Size 1 (2.25 mm) needles or size to obtain gauge

14 stitch markers

2 row counters (optional)

Crochet hook, size C/2 (2.75 mm)

gauge

44 sts and 28 rows = 4" in patt, blocked

lace pattern

(Multiple of 12 sts + plus 3 sts)

See chart on page 24 or follow the written directions below.

Row 1 (RS): Sl 1, knit to end.

Row 2 and all even-numbered rows: Sl 1, knit to end.

Rows 3, 5, 7, 9, 11, and 13 (RS): Sl 1, K1, pm, *K2tog twice, (YO, K1) 3 times, YO, ssk twice, K1, pm; rep from * to last st, K1.

Row 15: Sl 1, knit to end.

Row 16: Sl 1, knit to end.

shawl

CO 171 sts. Work 2 rows of garter st.

On next RS row, beg patt row 1 as follows: Sl 1, K1, pm, work 14 patt reps, placing a marker between each rep, K1. To keep track of your rows and vertical reps, try using 2 counters—1 for individual rows within a rep and 1 for the number of the rep you're currently working on.

Cont in patt, working 27 vertical reps.

Work 2 rows of garter st.

BO all sts loosely.

A FINE EDGE

Because the lace-weight yarn is so fine, you can give your shawl a nice, smooth, yet stretchy edge by slipping the first stitch of each row. Slip as if to purl on both right and wrong sides of the work. This is important for blocking.

finishing

To block lace, soak shawl overnight in cold water. Roll up in towel to remove excess moisture. On large, flat surface, pin out piece to finished dimensions. Ends will be deeply scalloped.

Fringe: Cut yarn into 120 pieces, 16" long. Using 4 pieces for each fringe, fold pieces in half lengthwise and use crochet hook to pull folded strands through edge of shawl at center of scallop. Loop ends through folded edge and pull tight—15 on each end of shawl.

DRAPED MOCK NECK TANK

draped mock neck tank

Such an easy, effortless style—this is a flattering fit for all.

By Melissa Matthay and Sheryl Thies

Skill Level: Beginner ◖◼▭▭▭

Sizes: XS (S, M, L, 1X, 2X)

Finished Bust Measurement: 33 (36, 38½, 41, 44, 46½)"

Finished Length to Outer Shoulder Edge: 17½ (19, 20, 21½, 23, 23)"

materials

375 (375, 425, 425, 475, 525) yds of bulky-weight cotton ribbon (**5**)

Size 13 (9 mm) needles, or size required to obtain gauge

US 13 (9 mm) circular needle (16") for neck

1 stitch holder

1 stitch marker

gauge

12 sts and 16 rows = 4" in St st

back

CO 50 (54, 58, 62, 66, 70) sts. Work in St st until piece measures 11 (12, 13, 14, 15, 15)".

Shape armholes: BO 2 (2, 3, 4, 5, 6) sts at beg of next 2 rows. Work dec row on EOR 5 (5, 6, 6, 7, 8) times as follows: K3, K2tog, knit to last 5 sts, ssk, K3—36 (40, 40, 42, 42, 42) sts.

Cont until piece measures 17½ (19, 20, 21½, 23, 23)" from beg.

Shape shoulders: BO 1 st at beg of each row 12 (16, 16, 18, 18, 18) times. Place rem 24 sts on holder.

front

Work as for back.

finishing

Sew shoulder and side seams. With circular needle, knit rem neck sts from holder, join, pm, and work in St st for 1½". BO all sts. Fold neck in half toward the inside and tack in place. Weave in ends.

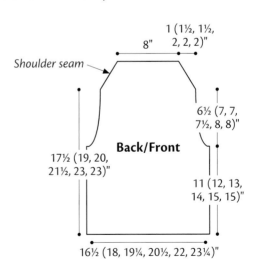

Shoulder seam

1 (1½, 1½, 2, 2, 2)"

8"

6½ (7, 7, 7½, 8, 8)"

17½ (19, 20, 21½, 23, 23)"

Back/Front

11 (12, 13, 14, 15, 15)"

16½ (18, 19¼, 20½, 22, 23¼)"

SHARK FIN TANK

shark fin tank

This tank top has an elegant drape and knit lace hem. Crochet edges provide a refined, feminine look.

By Melissa Matthay and Sheryl Thies

Skill Level: Intermediate ◼◼◼◻

Sizes: XS (S, M, L)

Finished Bust Measurement: 32 (35, 38½, 41½)"

Finished Length: 17 (19½, 21, 23)", excluding border

materials

500 (600, 600, 700) yds of worsted-weight woven cotton/rayon/polyester blend

Size 8 (5 mm) needles, or size required to obtain gauge

Crochet hook, size G/6 (4 mm)

gauge

20 sts and 24 rows = 4" in St st

lace border (make 2)

CO 8 sts. Knit 1 row. Work patt as follows:

Row 1 (RS): Sl 1 wyib, K1, (YO, K2tog) twice, YO, K2—9 sts.

Row 2: K2, YO, K2, (YO, K2tog) twice, K1—10 sts.

Row 3: Sl 1 wyib, K1, (YO, K2tog) twice, K2, YO, K2—11 sts.

Row 4: K2, YO, K4, (YO, K2tog) twice, K1—12 sts.

Row 5: Sl 1 wyib, K1, (YO, K2tog) twice, K4, YO, K2—13 sts.

Row 6: K2, YO, K6, (YO, K2tog) twice, K1—14 sts.

Row 7: Sl 1 wyib, K1, (YO, K2tog) twice, K6, YO, K2—15 sts.

Row 8: BO 7 sts, K2, (YO, K2tog) twice, K1—8 sts.

Rep rows 1–8 until border measures 16 (17½, 19¼, 20¾)". BO all sts.

back

On straight edge of border piece, PU 80 (88, 96, 104) sts and work in St st until piece measures 9 (10½, 12, 13½)" excluding border.

Shape armholes: BO 4 (4, 5, 6) sts at beg of next 2 rows, BO 2 (2, 4, 4) sts at beg of next 2 rows, dec 1 st at each edge EOR 4 (5, 5, 6) times—60 (66, 68, 72) sts. Cont until piece measures 11 (13, 14½, 16)" excluding border.

Shape neck: Work across 20 (22, 22, 23) sts, join second ball of yarn and BO center 20 (22, 24, 26) sts, finish row. Working both sides at same time, BO 3 sts at each neck edge once, dec 1 st at each neck edge EOR 5 (7, 7, 8) times.

Work rem 12 sts for each side until piece measures 17 (19½, 21, 23)" excluding border. BO all sts.

front

Work as for back.

finishing

Sew shoulder and side seams.

Neck edging: Using crochet hook, beg at right shoulder seam, work (1 dc, ch 1) around neck edge.

Armhole edging: Using crochet hook, beg at underarm seam, work (1 dc, ch 1) around each armhole.

Weave in ends.

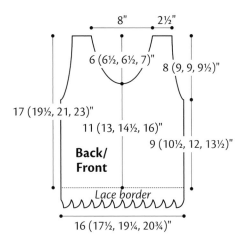

braided shell

A braided center cable accents this slenderizing shell. Can you be happy with just one?

By Melissa Matthay and Sheryl Thies

Skill Level: Intermediate ◖■■■◗

Sizes: XS (S, M, L, IX)

Finished Bust Measurement: 33 (36, 41, 44, 47)"

Finished Length: 19 (19, 20, 21, 22½)"

materials

275 (330 (390, 440, 500) yds of bulky-weight cotton/acrylic blend (5)

Size 13 (9 mm) circular needle, 24"

Size 15 (10 mm) needles or size required to obtain gauge

Cable needle

1 stitch holder

gauge

10 sts and 12 rows = 4" in braided cable patt on size 15 needles

braided cable

Rows 1, 5, and 9: K15 (17, 20, 22, 24), P1, K9, P1, K15 (17, 20, 22, 24).

Rows 2, 4, and 6: Knit the knit sts and purl the purl sts as they face you.

Row 3: K15 (17, 20, 22, 24), P1, sl 3 sts onto cn and hold in back, K3, K3 from cn, K3, P1, K15 (17, 20, 22, 24).

Row 7: K15 (17, 20, 22, 24), P1, K3, sl 3 sts onto cn and hold in front, K3, K3 from cn, P1, K15 (17, 20, 22, 24).

Row 8: Knit the knit sts and purl the purl sts as they face you.

Rep rows 1–8.

BRAIDED SHELL

back

With size 15 needles, CO 41 (45, 51, 55, 59) sts. Work in braided cable until piece measures 12 (12, 13, 13, 14)" from beg.

Shape armhole: BO 3 sts at beg of next 2 rows, dec 1 st at each edge EOR 4 (4, 5, 5, 5) times—27 (31, 35, 39, 43) sts.

Cont in patt until 19 (19, 20, 21, 22½)" from beg. BO all sts loosely.

front

Work as for back until 16 (16, 17, 18, 19½)" from beg.

Shape neck: Work in patt across 8 (10, 12, 14, 16) sts, place center 11 sts on holder, join second ball of yarn and finish row. Working both sides at same time, dec 1 st at each neck edge EOR 2 (3, 4, 4, 5) times—6 (7, 8, 10, 11) sts for each shoulder. Cont until 19 (19, 20, 21, 22½)" from beg. BO all sts loosely.

finishing

Sew shoulder seams tog.

Neckband: With size 13 circular needle, PU 21 sts along back neck edge, 6 (6, 8, 8, 8) sts along front neck edge, work center 11 sts from holder, PU 6 (6, 8, 8, 8) sts along front neck edge—44 (44, 48, 48, 48) sts. Join and work in K2, P2 rib for 7". BO loosely in patt.

Armhole bands: Sew side seams. PU 36 (36, 40, 40, 40) sts evenly around armhole. Join and work in K2, P2 rib for 1¼". BO loosely in patt.

Weave in ends.

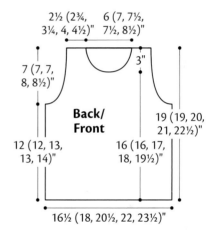

2½ (2¾, 3¼, 4, 4½)"

6 (7, 7½, 7½, 8½)"

3"

7 (7, 7, 8, 8½)"

Back/ Front

19 (19, 20, 21, 22½)"

12 (12, 13, 13, 14)"

16 (16, 17, 18, 19½)"

16½ (18, 20½, 22, 23½)"

graceful shell

Feel confident in this feminine shell with gracefully draped neckline.

By Melissa Matthay and Sheryl Thies

Skill Level: Easy ◼◼◻◻

Sizes: XS (S, M, L, IX)

Finished Bust Measurement: 34½ (37½, 40, 44, 46½)"

Finished Length: 19½ (19½, 21, 22½, 22½)"

materials

300 (300, 350, 400, 450) yds of bulky-weight rayon

Size 13 (9 mm) needles or size required to obtain gauge

Size 13 (9 mm) circular needle (24")

Optional: Crochet hook; size H/8 (5 mm)

1 stitch holder

1 stitch marker

gauge

12 sts and 15 rows = 4" in St st

back

CO 52 (56, 60, 66, 70) sts and work in St st until piece measures 12 (12, 13, 14, 14)" from beg.

Shape armhole: BO 3 (3, 4, 5, 5) sts at beg of next 2 rows, dec 1 st at each edge EOR 3 (3, 3, 4, 4) times—40 (44, 46, 48, 52) sts.

Cont until 19½ (19½, 21, 22½, 22½)" from beg. BO all sts loosely.

front

Work as for back until piece measures 14½ (14½, 15½, 17, 17)" from beg, ending with WS row.

Shape neck drape: K12 (14, 15, 15, 17) sts, M1, K16 (16, 16, 18, 18) sts, M1, K12 (14, 15, 15, 17) sts. This completes inc row. Rep inc row every 2 rows a total of 9 (9, 10, 10, 10) times; you will inc center sts by 2 with each inc row—58 (62, 66, 68, 72) sts.

Cont in patt until piece measures 19½ (19½, 21, 22½, 22½)" from beg. BO 12 (14, 15, 15, 17) sts at beg of next 2 rows. Place rem 34 (34, 36, 38, 38) sts on holder.

finishing

Sew shoulder seams.

Neckband: With RS facing you and circular needle, PU 22 sts around back neck edge, K34 (34, 36, 38, 38) sts from holder—56 (56, 58, 60, 60) sts. Join, pm, and knit for 1½". BO all sts loosely.

Sew side seams. Weave in ends.

Optional: Using crochet hook, work 1 rnd sc around each armhole edge.

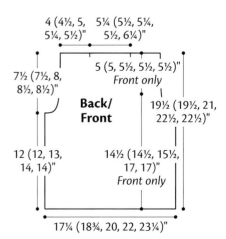

4 (4½, 5, 5¼, 5½)"   5¼ (5½, 5¼, 5½, 6¼)"

5 (5, 5½, 5½, 5½)"
Front only

7½ (7½, 8, 8½, 8½)"

Back/Front

19½ (19½, 21, 22½, 22½)"

12 (12, 13, 14, 14)"

14½ (14½, 15½, 17, 17)"
Front only

17¼ (18¾, 20, 22, 23¼)"

COLOR-BLOCK SHELL

color-block shell

Look and feel great in this shell with cool, pastel blocks outlined in black.

By Melissa Matthay and Sheryl Thies

Skill Level: Easy ◖◼☐◗

Sizes: XS (S, M, L, 1X)

Finished Bust Measurement: 37½ (39½, 41½, 43, 45)"

Finished Length: 19 (20, 21, 22½, 22½)"

materials

Worsted-weight cotton or cotton/rayon blend ④

A 70 yds in black

B 200 (200, 200, 300, 300) yds

C 200 (200, 200, 300, 300) yds

D 200 (200, 200, 300, 300) yds

E 200 (200, 200, 300, 300) yds

Size 9 (5.5 mm) needles or size required to obtain gauge

Size 7 (4.5 mm) circular needle (16") for neck and armholes

Crochet hook, size H/8 (5 mm)

gauge

17 sts and 21 rows = 4" in St st on larger needles

WORKING WITH TWO COLORS

To prevent holes, always pick up the new-color yarn from beneath the dropped yarn and keep the color just worked to the left.

back

With smaller needles and A, CO 80 (84, 88, 92, 96) sts and knit 1 row (WS row).

Change to larger needles and B, beg St st as follows: K40 (42, 44, 46, 48), drop B but do not cut yarn. Add C, K40 (42, 44, 46, 48). Work in St st and est colors until piece measures 10 (11, 12, 13, 13)" from beg, ending with WS row.

Change to A and knit 1 row. Change to D, cont in St st: Work 40 (42, 44, 46, 48) sts, drop D but do not cut yarn. Add E and work 40 (42, 44, 46, 48) sts. Cont in St st and est color until piece measures 11 (12, 13, 14, 14)" from beg, ending with WS row.

Shape armholes: BO 5 (5, 6, 6, 7) sts at beg of next 2 rows, dec 1 st at each edge EOR 6 (7, 8, 10, 10) times—58 (60, 60, 60, 62) sts. Cont in patt until piece measures 15½ (16½, 17½, 19, 19)" from beg, ending with WS row.

Shape neck: Work 21 (22, 22, 22, 23) sts, join second ball of yarn and BO center 16 sts, finish row. Working both sides at same time, at beg of each neck edge, BO 3 sts once, dec 1 st EOR 2 (3, 3, 3, 4) times—16 sts each shoulder.

Cont in patt until piece measures 19 (20, 21, 22½, 22½)" from beg. BO all sts.

front

Work as for back.

finishing

Black vertical chain on front and back:
Use crochet hook and 1 strand of A. With yarn underneath garment, insert hook into stitch between left and right colors on first row of A, wrap yarn around hook and pull loop through to RS (1 loop on hook). *Insert hook into next space above 2 strands of yarn of right-hand color, wrap yarn around hook and pull loop through to RS and through loop on hook (chain made). Rep from * to neck.

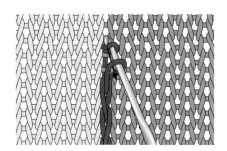

Sew shoulder and side seams.

Neck edging: With RS of garment facing you, smaller circular needle, and A, PU 88 (92, 92, 92 96) sts evenly around neck edge. Join and BO all sts loosely.

Armhole edging: With RS of garment facing you, smaller circular needle, and A, PU 74 (74, 76, 80, 80) sts evenly around armhole edge. Join and BO all sts loosely. Rep for second armhole.

Weave in ends. If necessary, block gently.

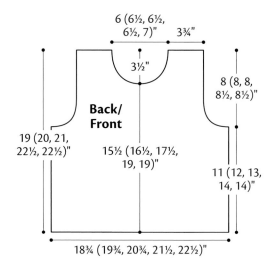

6 (6½, 6½, 6½, 7)"   3¾"

3½"

Back/Front

8 (8, 8, 8½, 8½)"

19 (20, 21, 22½, 22½)"   15½ (16½, 17½, 19, 19)"

11 (12, 13, 14, 14)"

18¾ (19¾, 20¾, 21½, 22½)"

dare-to-wear pink shell

When your wardrobe craves a little frill, we dare you to wear this pink scoop neck with ruffle trim. Go ahead, we double dare you!

By Melissa Matthay and Sheryl Thies

Skill Level: Easy ◖■□□

Sizes: XS (S, M, L, 1X)

Finished Bust Measurement: 37½ (37, 40, 42½, 44)"

Finished Length: 20 (21, 21, 22, 22)"

materials

450 (450, 450, 575, 575) yds of bulky-weight cotton/rayon/nylon blend (**5**)

Size 10½ (6.5 mm) circular needle (24") or size required to obtain gauge

1 stitch marker

gauge

12 sts and 16 rows = 4" in St st

back

CO 216 (224, 240, 256, 264) sts and work ruffle edge as follows:

Row 1: K2tog across—108 (112 120, 128, 132) sts.

Row 2: P2tog across—54 (56, 60, 64, 66) sts.

Work in St st until piece measures 12½ (13½, 13½, 14½, 14½)" from beg, ending with WS row.

Shape armholes: BO 4 sts at beg of next 2 rows. BO 2 sts at beg of next 2 rows. Dec 1 st at each edge EOR 2 (3, 4, 5, 6) times—38 (38, 40, 42, 42) sts.

Cont in St st until piece measures 20 (21, 21, 22, 22)" from beg. BO all sts.

DARE-TO-WEAR PINK SHELL

front

Work as for back until piece measures 13 (14, 14, 15, 15)" from beg, ending with WS row.

Cont with armhole shaping and AT SAME TIME shape neck as follows: Work across 17 (17, 18, 19, 19) sts, join second ball of yarn and BO center 4 sts, finish row. Working both sides at same time, at beg of each neck edge, BO 2 sts once, dec 1 st EOR 4 (4, 5, 5, 5) times—11 (11, 11, 12, 12) sts.

Cont in St st until piece measures 20 (21, 21, 22, 22)" from beg. BO all sts.

finishing

Sew shoulder and side seams.

Neck ruffle: With circular needle and WS facing you, PU 68 (68, 72, 72, 72) sts evenly along neck edge and join, pm.

Rnd 1: *K4, M1, rep from *—85 (85, 90, 90, 90) sts.

Rnd 2 and all even rnds: Knit.

Rnd 3: *K4, M1, rep from * to last 1 (1, 2, 2, 2) sts, knit to end—106 (106, 112, 112, 112) sts.

Rnd 5: *K4, M1, rep from * to last 2 (2, 0, 0, 0) sts, knit to end—132 (132, 140, 140, 140) sts.

Rnd 7: *K4, M1, rep from *—165 (165, 175, 175, 175) sts.

Rnd 9: *K1, M1, rep from *—330 (330, 350, 350, 350) sts.

Rnd 11: *K1, M1, rep from *—660 (660, 700, 700, 700) sts.

Rnd 13: K1f&b around—1320 (1320, 1400, 1400, 1400) sts. BO all sts.

finishing

Weave in ends. If necessary, block gently.

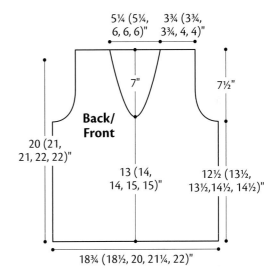

5¼ (5¼, 6, 6, 6)"   3¾ (3¾, 3¾, 4, 4)"

7"

7½"

Back/Front

20 (21, 21, 22, 22)"

13 (14, 14, 15, 15)"

12½ (13½, 13½, 14½, 14½)"

18¾ (18½, 20, 21¼, 22)"

LEAF-PRINT SHELL

leaf-print shell

This shell features a leaf pattern that looks like alternating leaves climbing up a stem.

By Julie Montanari

Skill Level: Intermediate ◼◼◼◻

Sizes: XS (S, M, L, 1X)

Finished Bust Measurement: 33 (36, 40, 44, 48)"

Finished Length: 16½ (18, 19, 19½, 20)"

materials

500 (600, 700, 800, 800) yds of bulky-weight acrylic/rayon/polyester blend ⑤

Size 10½ (6.5 mm) needles

Crochet hook, size I/9 (5.5 mm)

gauge

16 sts and 24 rows = 4" in patt

back

CO 71 (78, 86, 95, 103) sts. Work in patt as follows for your size (see Leaves and Stem chart [LS15] on page 44).

On all WS rows: Knit the knit sts and purl the purl sts as they face you.

XS: K1, P9, LS15, P3, LS15, P3, LS15, P9, K1.

S: K1, P5, LS15, P2, LS15, P2, LS15, P2, LS15, P5, K1.

M: K1, P9, LS15, P2, LS15, P2, LS15, P2, LS15, P9, K1.

L: K1, P12, LS15, P3, LS15, P3, LS15, P3, LS15, P12, K1.

1X: K1, P13, LS15, P5, LS15, P5, LS15, P5, LS15, P13, K1.

Cont in est patt until piece measures 10 (11, 11½, 11½, 11½)" from beg.

Shape armholes: BO 4 (2, 4, 6, 6) sts at beg of next 2 rows. Dec 1 st at each side next 5 (3, 5, 6, 7) RS rows—53 (68, 68, 71, 77) sts. Cont in est patt until piece measures 15½ (17, 18, 18½, 19)" from beg.

Shape neck: Work across 16 (21, 21, 22, 24) sts, join second ball of yarn, BO center 21 (26, 26, 27, 29) sts, finish row. Working both sides at same time, at each neck edge: BO 4 (5, 5, 5, 6) sts; 2 rows later, BO 4 (6, 6, 6, 6) sts.

Cont in est patt until piece measures 16½ (18, 19, 19½, 20)" from beg. BO rem 8 (10, 10, 11, 12) sts for each shoulder.

front

Work as for back until piece measures 14 (15½, 16½, 17, 17½)" from beg.

Shape neck: Work across 18 (24, 24, 25, 26) sts, join second ball of yarn, BO center 17 (20, 20, 21, 25) sts, finish row. Working both sides at same time, at each neck edge, BO 3 (5, 5, 5, 5) sts; 2 rows later, BO 3 (5, 5, 5, 5) sts; dec 1 st 4 times.

Cont in est patt until piece measures 16½ (18, 19, 19½, 20)" from beg. BO rem 8 (10, 10, 11, 12) sts for each shoulder.

finishing

Sew shoulder seams. Sew side seams.

Neck edging: Using crochet hook, work 1 rnd of sc around neck, beg and ending at center back.

Armhole edging: Using crochet hook, work 1 rnd of sc around both armholes, beg and ending at side seam.

Weave in ends.

Leaves and Stem (LS15)

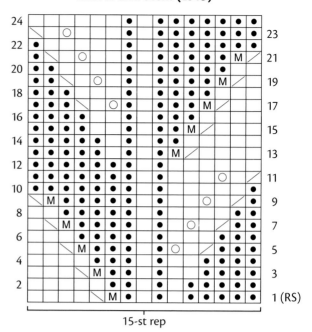

15-st rep

Key

- ● P on RS, K on WS
- ☐ K on RS, P on WS
- ◣ ssk
- ◿ K2tog
- M Make 1 st
- O Yarn over

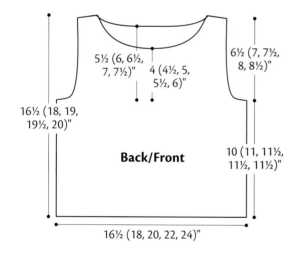

Back/Front

5½ (6, 6½, 7, 7½)"   4 (4½, 5, 5½, 6)"

6½ (7, 7½, 8, 8½)"

16½ (18, 19, 19½, 20)"

10 (11, 11½, 11½, 11½)"

16½ (18, 20, 22, 24)"

blue hawaii shell

This sweater—which combines a bottom lace panel and a lace turtleneck with a plain body—doubles as a dressy warm-weather top and an evening sweater.

By Carol Rasmussen Noble

Skill Level: Easy ◼◼☐☐

Sizes: To Fit Bust: 34 (38, 42, 46, 50)"

Finished Bust Measurement: 36½ (40½, 44½, 48½, 52½)"

Finished Length: 20½ (21, 21½, 22, 22½)"

materials

900 (1000, 1100, 1200, 1300) yards of light worsted-weight rayon/silk blend ❸

Size 4 (3.5 mm) needles or size to obtain gauge

Size 6 (3.5 mm) circular needle (16") for neck

1 stitch marker

gauge

20 sts and 32 rows = 4" in St st

patterns

See charts A and B on page 48 or follow the written directions below.

PATTERN A (chart on page 48)

(Multiple of 10 sts + 1 st)

Row 1 (RS): Ssk, *ssk, (YO, K1) 3 times, YO, K2tog, sl 1-K2tog-psso**; rep from * to ** 8 (9, 10, 11, 12) times; ssk, (YO, K1) 3 times, YO, (K2tog) twice.

Row 2 and all even rows: Purl.

Row 3: Ssk, *K3, YO, K1, YO, K3, sl 1-K2tog-psso**; rep from * to ** 8 (9, 10, 11, 12) times; K3, YO, K1, YO, K3, K2tog.

Row 5: Ssk, *K2, YO, K3, YO, K2, sl 1-K2tog-psso**; rep from * to ** 8 (9, 10, 11, 12) times; K2, YO, K3, YO, K2, K2tog.

Row 7: Ssk, *K1, YO, K5, YO, K1, sl 1-K2tog-psso**; rep from * to ** 8 (9, 10, 11, 12) times; K1, YO, K5, YO, K1, K2tog.

Row 9: Ssk, *YO, K1, YO, ssk, K1, K2tog, YO, K1, YO, sl 1-K2tog-psso**; rep from * to ** 8 (9, 10, 11, 12) times; YO, K1, YO, ssk, K1, K2tog, YO, K1, YO, K2tog.

Row 11: Ssk, *YO, K2, YO, sl 1-K2tog-psso, YO, K2, YO, sl 1-K2tog-psso**; rep from * to ** 8 (9, 10, 11, 12) times; YO, K2, YO, sl 1-K2tog-psso, YO, K2, YO, K2tog.

Row 13: K1, (YO, K3, sl 1-K2tog-psso, K3, YO, K1) 9 (10, 11, 12, 13) times.

Row 15: K1, (YO, K1, YO, K2tog, sl 1-K2tog-psso, ssk, YO, K1, YO, K1) 9 (10, 11, 12, 13) times.

BLUE HAWAII SHELL

Row 17: K1, (YO, K3, sl 1-K2tog-psso, K3, YO, K1) 9 (10, 11, 12, 13) times.

Row 19: K1, (K1, YO, K2, sl 1-K2tog-psso, K2, YO, K2) 9 (10, 11, 12, 13) times.

Row 21: K1, (K2, YO, K1, sl 1-K2tog-psso, K1, YO, K3) 9 (10, 11, 12, 13) times.

Row 23: K1, (K2tog, YO, K1, YO, sl 1-K2tog-psso, YO, K1, YO, ssk, K1) 9 (10, 11, 12, 13) times.

Row 25: K1, (YO, K3, sl 1-K2tog-psso, K3, YO, K1) 9 (10, 11, 12, 13) times.

Row 27: Ssk, *K3, YO, K1, YO, K3, sl 1-K2tog-psso**; rep from * to ** 8 (9, 10, 11, 12) times; K3, YO, K1, YO, K3, K2tog.

Row 28: Purl.

PATTERN B (chart on page 48)
(Multiple of 10 sts)

Row 1 (RS): *Ssk, (YO, K1) 3 times, YO, K2tog, sl 1-K2tog-psso; rep from * to end.

Row 2 and all even rows: Purl.

Row 3: *K3, YO, K1, YO, K3, sl 1-K2tog-psso; rep from * to end.

Row 5: *K2, YO, K3, YO, K2, sl 1-K2tog-psso; rep from * to end.

Row 7: *K1, YO, K5, YO, K1, sl 1-K2tog-psso; rep from * to end.

Row 9: *YO, K1, YO, ssk, K1, K2tog, YO, K1, YO, sl 1-K2tog-psso; rep from * to end.

Row 11: *YO, K2, YO, sl 1-K2tog-psso, YO, K2, YO, sl 1-K2tog-psso; rep from * to end.

Row 13: *YO, K3, sl 1-K2tog-psso, K3, YO, K1; rep from * to end.

Row 15: *YO, K1, YO, K2tog, sl 1-K2tog-psso, ssk, YO, K1, YO, K1; rep from * to end.

Row 17: *YO, K3, sl 1-K2tog-psso, K3, YO, K1; rep from * to end.

Row 19: *K1, YO, K2, sl 1-K2tog-psso, K2, YO, K2; rep from * to end.

Row 21: *K2, YO, K1, sl 1-K2tog-psso, K1, YO, K3; rep from * to end.

Row 23: *K2tog, YO, K1, YO, sl 1-K2tog-psso, YO, K1, YO, ssk, K1; rep from * to end.

Row 25: *YO, K3, sl 1-K2tog-psso, K3, YO, K1; rep from * to end.

Row 27: *K3, YO, K1, YO, K3, sl 1-K2tog-psso; rep from * to end.

Row 28: Purl.

back

With smaller straight needles, CO 91 (101, 111, 121, 131) sts. Knit 2 rows.

On next RS row, beg patt A following chart (page 48) or written instructions on page 45. From chart, work 1 beg st, 8 (9, 10, 11, 12) 10-st horizontal reps, and 10 end sts. Place markers between patt reps.

Work rows 1–28 of patt once, then work rows 1–10 once more.

Knit 2 rows.

On next RS row, beg St st. Work even in St st until piece measures 12½".

Beg with next RS row, work first and last 10 sts of each row in garter st, keeping body sts in St st. Rep for 8 rows total.

When piece measures 13½", BO 5 sts at beg of next 2 rows while maintaining 5 garter sts at each edge and body in St st.

Cont in patt until armhole measures 6½ (7, 7½, 8, 8½)".

On next RS row, work 15 (20, 25, 30, 35) sts; attach second ball of yarn and BO 49 sts for all sizes; work rem 15 (20, 25, 30, 35) sts in established patt. When armhole measures 7 (7½, 8, 8½, 9)", BO shoulder sts.

front

Work same as for back until armhole measures 3 (3½, 4, 4½, 5)". On next RS row, work 20 (25, 30, 35, 40) sts; attach 2nd ball of yarn and BO 39 sts for all sizes; work rem 20 (25, 30, 35, 40) sts in established patt.

On next and following RS rows, dec 1 st at each neck edge 5 times. When armhole measures 7 (7½, 8, 8½, 9)", BO shoulder sts.

finishing

Sew shoulder seams.

Neck: With circular needle, PU 90 sts evenly spaced around neck opening, beg at left shoulder. Join, pm, and work in St st for 10 rnds (knit all sts), then purl 1 rnd. Turn collar inside out to reverse the RS and WS, and work 9 horizontal reps from chart B or from written instructions on page 47. Work rows 1–28 of chart, then purl 1 rnd and BO all sts loosely kw.

Sew side seams.

Blocking: Soak overnight in cold water. Roll in towel to remove excess moisture. Lay out on flat surface and, stretching lace areas slightly, pin to given dimensions. When dry, remove pins.

Chart A

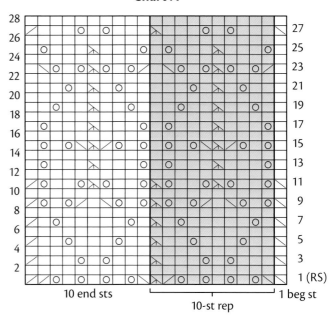

10 end sts   10-st rep   1 beg st

Chart B

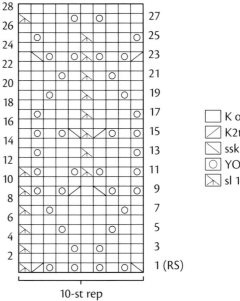

10-st rep

Key

☐	K on RS, P on WS
◩	K2tog
◪	ssk
◯	YO
⟁	sl 1-K2tog-psso

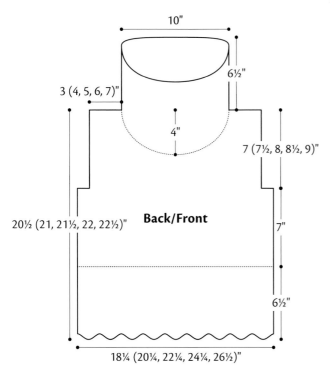

Back/Front

10"
6½"
3 (4, 5, 6, 7)"
4"
7 (7½, 8, 8½, 9)"
20½ (21, 21½, 22, 22½)"
7"
6½"
18¼ (20¼, 22¼, 24¼, 26½)"

butterfly tee

A dramatic pattern adorns a comfortable style. It's sure to become your favorite tee.

By Melissa Matthay and Sheryl Thies

Skill Level: Intermediate ◼◼◼▢

Sizes: S (M, L, IX)

Finished Bust Measurement: 35 (40, 44, 48)"

Finished Length: 18 (19, 20, 21)"

materials

725 (725, 900, 900) yds of worsted-weight 100% Egyptian cotton (**4**)

Size 8 (5 mm) needles or size required to obtain gauge

Size 7 (4.5 mm) needles

Size 7 (4.5 mm) circular needle (24") for neck

gauge

18 sts and 24 rows = 4" in patt A on larger needles

pattern stitches

PATTERN A (BUTTERFLY)
(Multiple of 10 sts + 9 sts)

Rows 1, 3, 5, 7, and 9 (RS): K2, *sl 5 wyif, K5, rep from *, end sl 5 wyif, K2.

Rows 2, 4, 6, and 8: Purl.

Row 10: P4; *on next st (which is center st of slipped group), insert right needle down through the 5 loose strands, bring needle up and transfer the 5 strands to left needle, purl the 5 strands with next st tog as 1 st, P9; rep from *, end P4.

Rows 11, 13, 15, 17, and 19: K7, *sl 5 wyif, K5; rep from *, end sl 5 wyif, K7.

Rows 12, 14, 16, and 18: Purl.

Row 20: P9, *insert needle down through 5 loose strands, bring them up and purl them tog with next st as before, P9; rep from * to end.

Rep rows 1–20.

PATTERN B
(Multiple of 6 sts + 7 [5, 9, 7] sts)

Row 1: K1 (0, 2, 1) sts, *K5, K1 wrapping yarn twice around needle; rep from *, end K6 (5, 7, 6) sts.

Row 2: P1 (0, 2, 1) sts, *P5, P1 dropping wrap; rep from *, end P6 (5, 7, 6) sts.

Rows 3 and 5: K1 (0, 2, 1) sts, *K5, sl 1 wyib; rep from *, end K6 (5, 7, 6) sts.

Rows 4 and 6: P1 (0, 2, 1) sts, *P5, sl 1 wyif; rep from *, end P6 (5, 7, 6) sts.

Row 7: K3 (2, 4, 3) sts, K1 wrapping yarn twice around needle, *K5, K1 wrapping yarn twice around needle; rep from *, end K3 (2, 4, 3) sts.

BUTTERFLY TEE

Row 8: P3 (2, 4, 3) sts, P1 dropping wrap, *P5, P1 (drop wrap); rep from *, end P3 (2, 4, 3) sts.

Rows 9 and 11: K3 (2, 4, 3) sts, sl 1 wyib, *K5, sl 1 wyib; rep from *, end K3 (2, 4, 3) sts.

Rows 10 and 12: P3 (2, 4, 3) sts, sl 1 wyif, *P5, sl 1 wyif; rep from *, end P3 (2, 4, 3) sts.

Rep rows 1–12.

back

With smaller needles, CO 79 (89, 99, 109) sts. Work in garter st for 6 rows.

Change to larger needles, beg patt A, and work for 40 (40, 60, 60) rows, completing 2 (2, 3, 3) 20-row reps of butterfly patt.

Beg patt B and work until piece measures 18 (19, 20, 21)" from beg. BO all sts.

front

Work as for back until piece measures 15 (16, 17, 18)" from beg.

Shape neck: Work in patt across 31 (36, 41, 46) sts, join second ball of yarn and BO center 17 sts, work in patt to end. Working both sides at same time, BO 4 sts at each neck edge once, BO 3 sts at each neck edge once, BO 2 sts at each neck edge once, dec 1 st at each neck edge once.

Work until piece measures 18 (19, 20, 21)" from beg. BO 21 (26, 31, 36) sts for each shoulder.

sleeves

With smaller needles, CO 69 (69, 79, 79) sts. Work in garter st for 6 rows.

Change to larger needles and work in patt A, completing rows 1–20 once.

Work in St st for 2 rows. BO all sts.

finishing

Sew shoulder seams.

Neckband: With circular needle, PU sts around neck edge, join, pm, and work in garter st for 6 rnds (in the rnd, that means knit 1 row, purl 1 row). BO all sts.

Sew sleeves to body. Sew sleeve and side seams. Weave in ends.

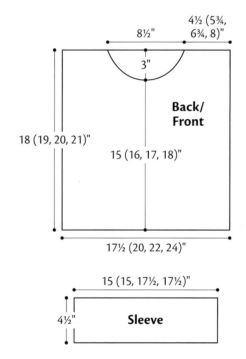

PULLOVERS

drop two pullover

The dropped stitches give this sweater its name. Worked side-to-side, it is the essence of exquisite simplicity and artfulness. Wear it over a camisole or black silk dress.

By Melissa Matthay and Sheryl Thies

Skill Level: Intermediate ⬤▮▮▯

Sizes: S (M, L)

Finished Bust Measurement: 40 (43, 46)"

Finished Length: 18½ (21, 23½)"

materials

Worsted-weight rayon/polyester blend

A 170 yds

C 170 yds

D 85 yds

DK-weight rayon/mohair/polyester blend

B 400 (400, 600) yds (2 strands held together throughout)

E 200 (200, 400) yds (2 strands held together throughout)

F 200 (200, 400) yds (2 strands held together throughout)

Size 9 (5.5 mm) needles or size required to obtain gauge

gauge

16 sts and 20 rows = 4" in St st with 2 strands of B, E, or F held tog

color stripe pattern

(Worked in St st)

Stripe 1: 4 rows of A

Stripe 2: 6 rows of B (2 strands of yarn held tog)

Stripe 3: 4 rows of C

Stripe 4: 1 row of D

Stripe 5: 4 rows of C

Stripe 6: 5 rows of E (2 strands of yarn held tog)

Stripe 7: 3 rows of B

Stripe 8: 4 rows of A

Stripe 9: 5 rows of F (2 strands of yarn held tog)

Rep 1–9 for stripe patt.

back

For S: With A, CO 46 sts. Beg with stripe 1, work 3 complete reps of color stripe.

For M: With B, CO 52 sts. Beg with stripe 7, work 3 complete reps of color stripe, then work stripes 7–9 once more.

For L: With D, CO 58 sts. Beg with stripe 4, work 3 complete reps of color stripe, then work stripes 4–9 once more.

BO row: *BO 4 sts, drop 2 sts, rep from * across to last 4 sts, BO rem sts. Let the dropped sts run completely to the opposite edge.

front

Work as for back.

sleeves

Beg with stripe 1 and follow color strip rep. *CO 5 sts for all sizes, work 2 rows in St st, rep from * until there are 40 sts on needle. Work in color stripe until larger edge (shoulder edge) measures 16 (18, 20)". **On next knit row, BO 4 sts, drop 2 sts, BO 1 st, knit to end of row. On next row, purl. Rep from ** until 3 sts rem. BO rem sts.

finishing

Sew 5" shoulder seams. Sew in sleeves. Sew sleeve and side seams. Weave in ends.

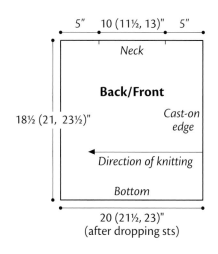

5"   10 (11½, 13)"   5"

Neck

Back/Front

Cast-on edge

18½ (21, 23½)"

← Direction of knitting

Bottom

20 (21½, 23)"
(after dropping sts)

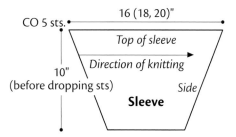

CO 5 sts.   16 (18, 20)"

Top of sleeve

→ Direction of knitting

10"
(before dropping sts)

Side

Sleeve

creating a laddered effect

Dropping the stitches creates the laddering effect and will dramatically elongate the knit piece. Be sure to let the dropped stitches run all the way to the cast-on edge. The bind-off stitches over the dropped stitches must be loose enough to accommodate the length of the ladders.

1. Bind off normally up to the stitches to be dropped. Make the bind-off loop on the right needle large. Drop two stitches and let them unravel.

2. Unravel the two stitches to the cast-on edge. Adjust the bind-off loop to span the distance to the next stitch over the dropped stitches.

3. Complete the bind-off over the dropped stitches.

4. Bind off normally. The area where the stitches were dropped should not be pulled or puckered and the laddering should be even.

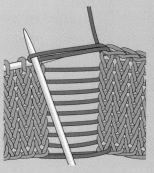

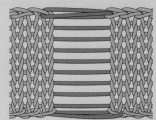

soft-twist tunic

The bottom of this tunic is ribbed, and nine-stitch cables are worked in a staggered pattern to pull the fabric in and create the A-line shape. A soft mohair yarn is a great choice. Expect to use needles a few sizes up from the recommended size on the yarn label.

By Julie Montanari

Skill Level: Intermediate

Sizes: XS (S, M, L, IX)

Finished Bust Measurement: 33 (36, 40, 44, 48)"

Finished Length: 24½ (26, 27½, 28, 28½)"

materials

1625 (1825, 2075, 2275, 2450) yds of DK-weight kid mohair/nylon blend **3**

Size 9 (5.5 mm) needles

Cable needle

gauge

21 sts and 21 rows = 4" in soft twist patt (chart on page 59)

pattern stitches

TRIPLE RIB (chart on page 59)

(Multiple of 6 sts + 5 sts)

Row 1 (RS): K1, *(K1, P1) 3 times, rep from * to last 4 sts, end K1, P1, K2.

Row 2: K1, P3, *K3, P3, rep from * to last st, end K1.

Rep rows 1 and 2.

TRIPLE RIB WITH BORDER (chart on page 59)

(Multiple of 6 sts + 7 sts)

Row 1 (RS): K1, (K1, P1) twice, *K1, P1, rep from * to last 2 sts, end K2.

Row 2: K1, P1, *K3, P3, rep from * to last 5 sts, end K3, P1, K1.

Rep rows 1 and 2.

back

T9 (Twist 9 sts): Sl 6 sts to cn and hold at front, work next 3 sts as (K1, P1, K1), sl 3 sts from cn back to left needle and work as (P1, K1, P1), work last 3 sts from cn as (K1, P1, K1).

CO 95 (103, 107, 119, 131) sts.

SOFT-TWIST TUNIC

For XS (M, L, 1X): Work in triple rib patt.

For S: Work in triple rib with border patt.

Work in appropriate patt to approx 4½ (5½, 6½, 6½)" from beg, ending with WS row. Work 19 (23, 25, 31, 37) sts in triple rib patt, T9, work 39 sts in est patt, T9, work in patt to end of row. Work in est ribbing patts without T9 for 15 more rows. On next RS row, work 19 (23, 25, 31, 37) sts in patt, T9, work 15 sts in patt, T9, work 15 sts in patt, T9, work to end of row. Work another 15 rows in est rib patts without T9. On next RS row, beg soft-twist chart on page 59 as follows:

For XS (S, M): Work 7 (11, 13) sts in est patt, start soft-twist chart at row 9, work 24-st rep 3 times, work final cable sts as indicated on chart, work rem 7 (11, 13) sts in est patt.

For L (1X): Work 7 (13) sts in est patt, start soft-twist chart at row 1, work 24-st rep 4 times, work final cable sts as indicated on chart, work rem 7 (13) sts in est patt.

Cont in est patts until piece measures 15½ (16½, 17½, 17½, 17½)" from beg.

Shape armholes: BO 2 (2, 4, 2, 6) sts at beg of next 2 rows. Dec 1 st at each side next 2 (2, 2, 2, 4) RS rows—87 (95, 95, 111, 111) sts. Note that the different sizes have different edges:

For XS: Work edge with (K2, P1) on outside of first and last (7th) cable.

For S and M: Work edge with K1, 6 sts of est rib on outside of first and last (7th) cable.

For L and 1X: Work edge with (K2, P1) on outside of first and last (9th) cable.

Cont in est patt until piece measures 23½ (25, 26½, 27, 27½)" from beg.

Shape neck: Work 29 (31, 31, 37, 37) sts in est patt, join second ball of yarn, BO center 29 (33, 33, 37, 37) sts, finish row. Working both sides at same time, at each neck edge, BO 4 (4, 4, 5, 5) sts; 2 rows later, BO 4 (4, 4, 5, 5) sts; 2 rows later, BO 3 (4, 4, 5, 5) sts.

Cont neck shaping and AT SAME TIME shape shoulders when piece measures 24 (25½, 27, 27½, 28)".

Shape shoulders: At each shoulder edge, BO 6 (6, 6, 7, 7) sts; 2 rows later, BO 6 (7, 7, 8, 8) sts; 2 rows later, BO rem 6 (6, 6, 7, 7) sts.

front

Work as for back until piece measures 15½ (16½, 17½, 17½, 17½)" from beg.

Work armhole shaping as for back. AT SAME TIME, work until fourth cable cross of center cable (approx 1" above armhole). On next WS row, dec 1 st at center. On next RS row, work to center cable (which now has 8 sts). Work first 4 sts as (K1, P1, K2). These 4 sts are now the left front neckband. Join second ball of yarn. Work rem sts of center cable as (K2, P1, K1) (the right front neckband). Cont in patt, working 2 front sides separately—43 (47, 47, 55, 55) sts each side. AT SAME TIME, dec 1 st (just inside neckband) at each neck edge next 10 RS rows. Dec 1 st at each neck edge 10 (13, 13, 18, 18) more times, evenly spaced until piece measures 24 (25½, 27, 27½, 28)" from beg.

Shape shoulders: At each shoulder edge, BO 6 (6, 6, 7, 7) sts; 2 rows later, BO 6 (7, 7, 8, 8) sts; 2 rows later, BO 6 (6, 6, 7, 7) sts. Cont working rem 5 sts as (K5, K1, P1, K1, K5) until neckbands are long enough to meet in center back.

sleeves

CO 47 (47, 59, 59, 59) sts. Work in triple rib patt for 3"; then work cable cuff chart for 12 rows.

Cont in triple rib patt, inc 1 st at each side 10 (14, 13, 16, 19) times, evenly spaced between top of cuff and 17½ (18½, 19, 19, 19)"—67 (75, 85, 91, 97) sts.

Shape cap: BO 4 (4, 5, 5, 6) sts at beg of next 2 rows. Dec 1 st at each side of each RS row until sleeve cap measures 4½ (4½, 4½, 5, 5½)". BO 2 sts at beg of each row until sleeve cap measures 5 (5½, 6, 6½, 6½)". BO rem sts.

finishing

Sew shoulder seams. Sew neckbands to back neck. Sew neckbands tog at center back. Sew in sleeves. Weave in ends.

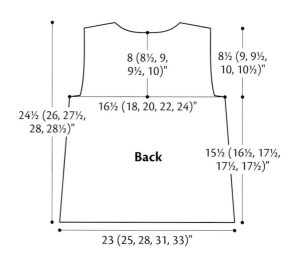

8 (8½, 9, 9½, 10)"

8½ (9, 9½, 10, 10½)"

24½ (26, 27½, 28, 28½)"

16½ (18, 20, 22, 24)"

Back

15½ (16½, 17½, 17½, 17½)"

23 (25, 28, 31, 33)"

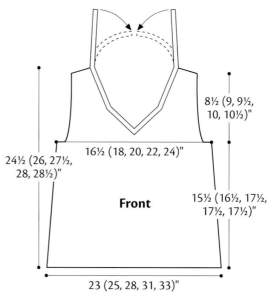

8½ (9, 9½, 10, 10½)"

24½ (26, 27½, 28, 28½)"

16½ (18, 20, 22, 24)"

Front

15½ (16½, 17½, 17½, 17½)"

23 (25, 28, 31, 33)"

Neckband extensions are knit straight out from front shoulder and sewn down to curve of back neck.

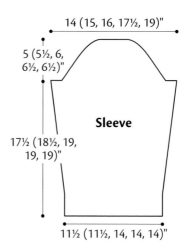

14 (15, 16, 17½, 19)"

5 (5½, 6, 6½, 6½)"

Sleeve

17½ (18½, 19, 19, 19)"

11½ (11½, 14, 14, 14)"

Triple Rib

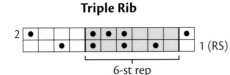

6-st rep

Triple Rib with Border

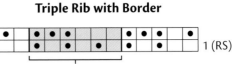

6-st rep

Soft Twist

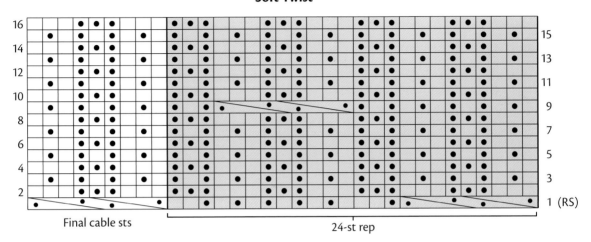

Final cable sts

24-st rep

Cable Cuff

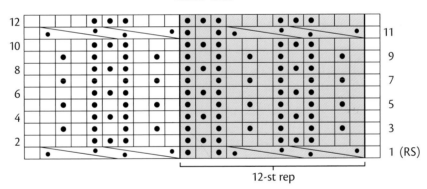

12-st rep

Key

☐ K on RS, P on WS

● P on RS, K on WS

Sl 6 sts to cn and hold in front, work next 3 sts as K1, P1, K1, sl 3 sts back to left needle and work as P1, K1, P1, work last 3 sts from cn as K1, P1, K1.

TWISTED-YOKE PULLOVER

twisted-yoke pullover

This pattern calls for a smooth yarn in a DK weight and is worked with two strands held together throughout. A heavier-weight yarn, worked in a single strand, would also look great.

By Julie Montanari

Skill Level: Intermediate ◖◼◼◻

Sizes: XS (S, M, L, lX)

Finished Bust Measurement: 33 (36, 40, 44, 48)"

Finished Length: 18½ (20, 21, 21½, 22½)"

materials

1075 (1175, 1375, 1500, 1675) yds of DK-weight silk/cashmere blend (worked with 2 strands held tog) **3**

US 10½ (6.5 mm) needles or size required to obtain gauge

2 stitch holders

gauge

16 sts and 22 rows = 4" in patt with 2 strands of DK-weight yarn held tog, or 1 strand of worsted-weight yarn

pattern stitches

MISTAKE RIB (chart on page 63)

(Multiple of 4 sts + 3 sts)

Row 1 (RS): K2, (P2, K2) to last st, K1.

Row 2: K1, *P1, K2, P1, rep from * to last 2 sts, P1, K1

Rep rows 1 and 2.

BROKEN TWISTED RIB (chart on page 63)

(Multiple of 4 sts + 3 sts)

Row 1 (RS): K1, purl to last st, K1.

Row 2: K1 *P1, K1, rep from * to last 2 sts, P1, K1.

Row 3: K1, K1tbl, *P1, K1tbl, rep from * to last st, K1.

Row 4: As row 2.

Row 5: As row 1.

Row 6: K1, *K1, P1, rep from * to last 2 sts, K2.

Row 7: K1, P1, *K1tbl, P1, rep from * to last st, K1.

Row 8: As row 6.

Rep rows 1–8.

back

With 2 strands of yarn held tog, CO 67 (75, 83, 91, 99) sts.

Work in mistake rib until piece measures 10½ (11½, 12, 12, 12)" from beg.

Shape armholes: BO 5 (5, 5, 7, 7) sts at beg of next 2 rows. Dec 1 st at each side on next 3 (3, 3, 5, 5) RS rows—51 (59, 67, 67, 75) sts rem. At 1" past armhole, beg with RS row, change to broken twisted rib, and work until armhole measures 7 (7½, 8, 8½, 9½)".

Shape neck: Work across 15 (19, 20, 20, 22) sts, move center 21 (21, 27, 27, 31) sts to holder, join second ball of yarn, finish row. Working both sides at same time, dec 1 st at each neck edge on next 3 RS rows. AT SAME TIME, when armhole measures 7½ (8, 8½, 9, 10)", shape shoulders.

Shape shoulders: At each shoulder edge, BO 6 (8, 8, 8, 9) sts; 2 rows later, BO rem 6 (8, 9, 9, 10) sts.

front

Work as for back until piece measures 16 (17, 18, 18½, 19½)" from beg.

Shape neck: Work across 20 (24, 26, 26, 28) sts, move center 11 (11, 15, 15, 19) sts to holder, join second ball of yarn, finish row. Working both sides at same time, at each neck edge, BO 2 sts; 2 rows later, BO 2 sts; dec 1 st next 4 (4, 5, 5, 5) RS rows.

AT SAME TIME, when armhole measures 7½ (8, 8½, 9, 10)", work shoulder shaping as for back.

sleeves

With 2 strands of yarn held tog, CO 33 (37, 41, 49, 53) sts.

Set up patt as follows: Knit 1 row on WS. On next (RS) row, switch to broken twisted rib, starting with row 1. Inc 1 st on each side in row 6 of cuff patt. Work a total of 13 rows of broken twisted rib, ending with row 5 (RS).

Switch to mistake rib, starting with row 2 (WS). On next RS row, inc 1 st at each side. Inc 1 st at each side 8 more times, evenly spaced between cuff and 10"—53 (57, 61, 69, 73) sts.

Shape cap: BO 4 (4, 4, 5, 5) sts at beg of next 2 rows. Dec 1 st at each side of each RS row until sleeve cap measures 4½ (4½, 4½, 5, 5½)". BO 2 sts at beg of each row until sleeve cap measures 5½ (5½, 6, 6½, 7)". BO rem sts.

finishing

Sew shoulder seam for one shoulder.

Collar: With RS facing you, PU collar sts as follows (give or take 1 or 2): 5 sts from back side neck, 21 (21, 27, 27, 31) sts from back holder, 5 sts from back side neck, 13 sts from front side neck, 11 (11, 15, 15, 19) sts from front holder, 13 sts from front side neck—68 (68, 78, 78, 86) sts total. On next row (WS), knit across. ON NEXT ROW, inc or dec 1 or 2 sts to achieve total number of sts equal to a multiple of 4 plus 3 (for example, 67, 71, 75, 79, 83, 87). Switch to mistake rib. For a turtleneck, remember that inside of sweater body will fold over and become RS of turtleneck. Work for 5" (or desired length). BO very loosely.

Sew seam for second shoulder, and for collar. Sew in sleeves. Sew side seams and sleeve seams. Weave in ends.

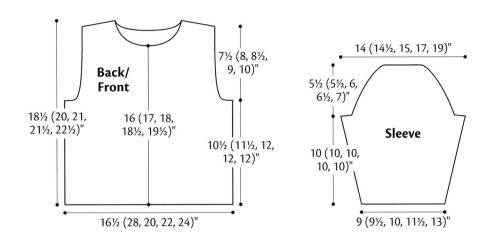

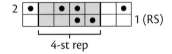

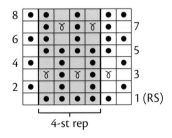

four corners pullover

Whatever your angle, you'll be right with this versatile pullover. It can be worn as a beach cover-up or over dressy slacks with pearls for an evening out.

By Melissa Matthay and Sheryl Thies

Skill Level: Beginner ◖■■▷

Sizes: S (M, L, 1X)

Finished Bust Measurement: 36 (39, 43½, 46½)"

Finished Length: 20 (21, 25, 26)"

materials

600 (650, 700, 750) yds of bulky-weight acrylic/polyamid blend (5)

Size 13 (9 mm) needles or size required to obtain gauge

Crochet hook, size I/9 (5.5 mm)

gauge

11 sts and 16 rows = 4" in St st

patterns

PATTERN A

Row 1: K25 (27, 30, 32) sts, P25 (27, 30, 32) sts.

Row 2: Knit the knit sts and purl the purl sts as they face you.

Rep row 2.

PATTERN B

Row 1: P25 (27, 30, 32) sts, K25 (27, 30, 32) sts.

Row 2: Knit the knit sts and purl the purl sts as they face you.

Rep row 2.

back

With size 13 needles, CO 50 (54, 60, 64) sts.

Work in patt A until piece measures 11 (12, 13, 14)" from beg.

Work in patt B until piece measures 20 (21, 25, 26)" from beg. BO all sts loosely.

front

Work as for back until piece measures 17 (18, 22, 23)" from beg.

Shape neck: Work across 18 (20, 23, 25) sts, join a second ball of yarn and BO center 14 sts, work across rem 18 (20, 23, 25) sts. Working both sides at same time, BO 2 sts at each neck edge once, dec 1 st at each neck edge EOR 2 times—14 (16, 19, 21) sts each shoulder.

Cont in patt until each side measures 20 (21, 25, 26)" from beg. BO rem sts.

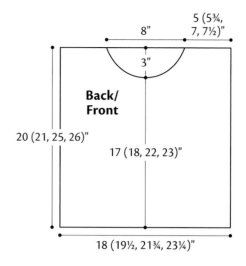

sleeves

CO 30 sts, work in St st for 6 rows.

Cont in St st, inc 1 st at each edge every 6 rows 11 times—52 sts. For better seams, make inc 2 sts from each edge.

Cont until piece measures 17" or desired length. BO 4 sts at beg of next 10 rows. BO 12 rem sts.

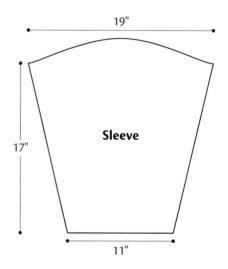

finishing

Sew shoulder seams. Sew seam on one sleeve with knit side out. Sew seam on the other sleeve with purl side out. Sew side seams, leaving a 6" opening at the bottom edge on each side for slit. Sew in sleeves.

Slit edging: PU sts around slit edge and BO.

Neck edging: Using crochet hook, work 1 row of sc around neck edge.

Weave in ends.

cashmere-and-silk fitted cowl

The lines of this cowl-neck top drape gracefully. It can be worn under a business suit for a day in the office or alone as a dressy sweater.

By Carol Rasmussen Noble

Skill Level: Easy ⬛⬛◻◻

Sizes: M (L, 1X, 2X, 3X)

Finished Bust Measurement: 44 (48, 52, 56, 60)"

Finished Length: 25½ (26, 26½, 27, 27½)"

materials

1350 (1600, 1825, 1050, 2300) yds of fingering-weight cashmere/silk blend [1]

Size 2 (2.75 mm) needles or size required to obtain gauge

Set of size 2 (2.75 mm) double-pointed needles for neck
1 stitch marker

gauge

20 sts and 32 rows = 4" in double seed st

double seed stitch

(Multiple of 4 sts)

Row 1 (RS): *K2, P2, rep from *.

Row 2: *P2, K2, rep from *.

Row 3: *P2, K2, rep from *.

Row 4: *K2, P2, rep from *.

Rep rows 1–4.

back

CO 110 (120, 130, 140, 150) sts. Work in double seed st patt for 4", ending on a WS row.

On next RS row, dec 1 st at each edge, then dec 1 st at each edge on RS row every 8 rows 4 times (5 sts dec at each edge).

At 9" on RS, inc 1 st at each edge, and then inc 1 st at each edge on RS row every 8 rows 4 times (5 sts inc at each edge). Cont in patt for 3", ending on a WS row.

Shape armholes: At beg of next 2 rows, BO 10 sts—90 (100, 110, 120, 130) sts. Cont in patt until back measures 24½ (25, 25½, 26, 26½)" from beg.

Shape neck and shoulders: Work 25 (27, 29, 32, 34) sts in patt, attach second ball of yarn and BO 40 (46, 52, 56, 62) sts, finish row. Working each side separately, dec 1 st at each neck edge on following RS row twice—23 (25, 27, 30, 32) sts.

CASHMERE-AND-SILK FITTED COWL

Cont in patt until back measures 25½ (26, 26½, 27, 27½)" from beg. BO all sts loosely.

front

Work same as back until armhole measures 6¼ (6½, 6¾, 7, 7¼)", ending on a WS row.

Shape neck and shoulders: On next RS row, work 33 (35, 37, 40, 42) sts, attach second ball of yarn and BO 24 (30, 36, 40, 46) sts finish row. Working each side separately, dec as follows for all sizes: BO 2 sts each neck edge EOR 3 times, and then dec 1 st each neck edge EOR 4 times—23 (25, 27, 30, 32) sts for each shoulder.

Cont in patt until front measures 25½ (26, 26½, 27, 27½)" from beg. BO all sts loosely.

sleeves

CO 40 (40, 45, 45, 50) sts. Working in patt, on fifth and every subsequent fourth row (RS), inc 1 st at each edge 27 (30, 30, 32, 32) times—94 (100, 105, 109, 114) sts.

Cont in patt until sleeve measures 20½ (21, 21½, 22, 22½)" from beg. BO all sts loosely.

finishing

Sew shoulder seams.

Cowl: With dpns, starting at left shoulder pick up 1 of every 2 sts on diagonal edges; 2 of every 3 sts on front neck BO; 3 of every 4 sts on back neck BO. Patt requires multiple of 4 sts. Make any necessary adjustments (inc or dec) on left shoulder. Join, pm, and work in patt in the rnd until cowl measures 12" for all sizes. BO all sts very loosely in patt.

Sew in sleeves. Sew side and sleeve seams. Weave in ends. No blocking is necessary. Do not steam, as this will flatten the patt.

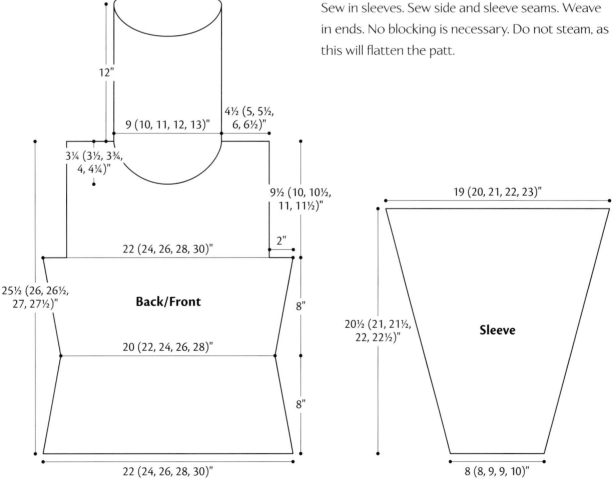

FUCHSIA PULLOVER

fuchsia pullover

Just like the flower, this comfortable-fitting pullover will be a perennial favorite. The Fuchsia pattern is very easy and enjoyable to work.

By Melissa Matthay and Sheryl Thies

Skill Level: Easy ◼◼◻◻

Sizes: XS (S, M, L, 1X)

Finished Bust Measurement: 36 (40, 44, 48, 52)"

Finished Length: 22 (24¾, 24¾, 27½, 27½)"

materials

750 (875, 1000, 1125, 1250) yds of bulky-weight wool/mohair ⑤

Size 10½ (6.5 mm) needles or size required to obtain gauge

Size 10 (6 mm) circular needle (24") for neck

1 stitch holder

1 stitch marker

gauge

12 sts and 17½ rows = 4" in fuchsia patt on larger needles after blocking

fuchsia pattern

The fuchsia patt has st incs in rows 1, 3, and 5; the corresponding decs are in rows 7, 9, and 11. Only count the number of sts after row 11 or 12.

BACK AND FORTH (Multiple of 6 sts)

Row 1 (RS): *P2, K2, YO, P2, rep from *.

Row 2: *K2, P3, K2, rep from *.

Row 3: *P2, K3, YO, P2, rep from *.

Row 4: *K2, P4, K2, rep from *.

Row 5: *P2, K4, YO, P2, rep from *.

Row 6: *K2, P5, K2, rep from *.

Row 7: *P2, K3, K2tog, P2, rep from *.

Row 8: Rep row 4.

Row 9: *P2, K2, K2tog, P2, rep from *.

Row 10: Rep row 2.

Row 11: *P2, K1, K2tog, P2, rep from *.

Row 12: *K2, P2, K2, rep from *.

Rep rows 1–12.

IN THE ROUND (Multiple of 6 sts)

Rnd 1: *K2, YO, P4, rep from *.

Rnd 2: *K3, P4, rep from *.

Rnd 3: *K3, YO, P4, rep from *.

Rnd 4: *K4, P4, rep from *.

Rnd 5: *K4, YO, P4, rep from *.

Rnd 6: *K5, P4, rep from *.

Rnd 7: *K3, K2tog, P4, rep from *.

Rnd 8: *K4, P4, rep from *.

Rnd 9: *K2, K2tog, P4, rep from *.

Rnd 10: *K3, P4, rep from *.

Rnd 11: *K1, K2tog, P4, rep from *.

Rnd 12: *K2, P4, rep from *.

Rep rnds 1–12.

back

With larger needles, CO 54 (60, 66, 72, 78) sts and work fuchsia patt *back and forth* until piece measures approx 13¾ (16½, 16½, 19¼, 19¼)", ending with row 12.

Shape armholes: BO 6 sts at beg of next 2 rows—42 (48, 54, 60, 66) sts.

Cont in patt until piece measures 22 (24¾, 24¾, 27½, 27½)" from beg. BO all sts in patt.

front

Work as for back until piece measures 19¼ (22, 22, 24¾, 24¾)", ending with row 12.

Shape neck: Work 9 (12, 15, 18, 21) sts, place center 24 sts on holder, join second ball of yarn and finish row. Working both sides at same time, at each neck edge, dec 1 st EOR 2 times—7 (10, 13, 16, 19) sts each shoulder.

Cont in patt until piece measures 22 (24¾, 24¾, 27½, 27½)" from beg. BO all sts in patt.

sleeves

With larger needles, CO 24 (24, 24, 30, 30) sts and work fuchsia patt *back and forth*, inc 1 st at each edge every 6 rows 13 (13, 13, 10, 10) times—50 sts. For better seams, work inc 2 sts from edge.

Cont in patt until piece measures 19¼" or desired length, ending with row 12. BO rem sts loosely.

finishing

Sew shoulder seams.

Collar: With smaller circular needle and RS facing you, PU 22 sts along back neck, 7 sts down left front, 24 sts from holder, 7 sts up right front—60 sts. Join, pm, and work in fuchsia patt *in the rnd* for 12 rows. BO loosely in patt.

Sew in sleeves. Sew sleeve and side seams. Weave in ends. Block gently.

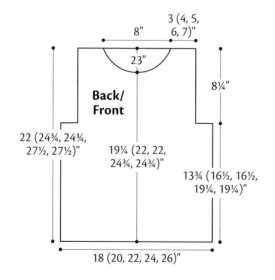

8"

3 (4, 5, 6, 7)"

23"

8¼"

Back/Front

22 (24¾, 24¾, 27½, 27½)"

19¼ (22, 22, 24¾, 24¾)"

13¾ (16½, 16½, 19¼, 19¼)"

18 (20, 22, 24, 26)"

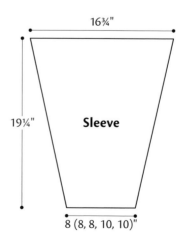

16¾"

19¼"

Sleeve

8 (8, 8, 10, 10)"

romantic ruffle pullover

Accented with a ruffle trim and center lace panel, this buttery-soft pullover will appeal to your romantic side.

By Melissa Matthay and Sheryl Thies

Skill Level: Intermediate ◖◼◼◻

Sizes: XS (S, M, L, IX)

Finished Bust Measurement: 37 (39½, 41½, 43½, 46)"

Finished Length: 20 (20, 21, 22½, 22½)"

materials

875 (1000, 1000, 1125, 1250) yds of worsted-weight kid mohair/wool blend (**4**)

Size 10 (6 mm) needles or size required to obtain gauge

Size 10 (6 mm) circular needle (24")

Size 8 (5 mm) circular needle (24")

2 stitch markers

gauge

15 sts and 19 rows = 4" in St st on larger needles

CENTER LACE PATTERN
(Worked over 18 sts)

Row 1 (RS): P2, YO, K3, ssk, K9, P2.

Row 2 and all WS rows: K2, P14, K2.

Row 3: P2, K1, YO, K3, ssk, K8, P2.

Row 5: P2, K2, YO, K3, ssk, K7, P2.

Row 7: P2, K3, YO, K3, ssk, K6, P2.

Row 9: P2, K4, YO, K3, ssk, K5, P2.

Row 11: P2, K5, YO, K3, ssk, K4, P2.

Row 13: P2, K6, YO, K3, ssk, K3, P2.

Row 15: P2, K7, YO, K3, ssk, K2, P2.

Row 17: P2, K8, YO, K3, ssk, K1, P2.

Row 19: P2, K9, YO, K3, ssk, P2.

Row 21: P2, K14, P2.

Row 22: K2, P14, K2.

Rep rows 1–22.

back

With larger needles, CO 210 (222, 234, 246, 258) sts. Work (K1, K2tog) across row—140 (148, 156, 164, 172) sts.

Next row: P2tog across row—70 (74, 78, 82, 86) sts.

Change to smaller needles and work in K1, P1 ribbing for 2", ending with WS row.

ROMANTIC RUFFLE PULLOVER

Change to larger needles and work setup row: 26 (28, 30, 32, 34) sts in St st, pm, 18 sts in center lace patt, pm, 26 (28, 30, 32, 34) sts in St st. Cont in est patt until piece measures 12 (12, 13, 14, 14)" from beg, ending with WS row.

Shape armholes: BO 4 sts at beg of next 2 rows. Dec 1 st at each armhole edge EOR 4 (4, 6, 6, 8) times—54 (58, 58, 62, 62) sts.

Cont in patt until piece measures 20 (20, 21, 22½, 22½)" from beg. BO all sts in patt.

front

Work as for back until piece measures 17 (17, 18, 19½, 19½)" from beg, ending with WS row.

Shape neck: Work across 20 (22, 22, 23, 23) sts, join second ball of yarn and BO center 14 (14, 14, 16, 16) sts, finish row. Working both sides at same time, at each neck edge, BO 3 sts once, BO 2 sts once, dec 1 st at each neck edge EOR 1 (1, 1, 2, 2) times—14 (16, 16, 16, 16) sts each shoulder.

Cont in patt until piece measures 20 (20, 21, 22½, 22½)" from beg. BO all sts in patt.

sleeves

With larger needles, CO 96 (96, 96, 108, 108) sts and work (K1, K2tog) across row—64 (64, 64, 72, 72) sts.

Next row: P2tog across row—32 (32, 32, 36, 36) sts.

Change to smaller needles and work in K1, P1 ribbing for 2", inc 2 sts evenly across last WS row—34 (34, 34, 38, 38) sts.

Change to larger needles and work setup row: 8 (8, 8, 10, 10) sts in St st, pm, 18 sts in center lace patt, pm, 8 (8, 8, 10, 10) sts in St st. Cont in est patt, inc 1 st at each edge every 4 rows 5 times, then inc 1 st at each edge every 6 rows 4 times—52 (52, 52, 56, 56) sts. Cont in patt until piece measures 17" or desired length.

Shape cap: BO 4 sts at beg of next 2 rows, dec 1 st at each edge EOR 15 times. BO rem 14 (14, 14, 18, 18) sts.

finishing

Sew shoulder seams.

Collar: With smaller circular needle and RS facing you, PU 62 (62, 62, 66, 66) sts evenly around neck edge. Join, pm, and work in K1, P1 ribbing for 7". Change to larger circular needle and work ruffle edge as follows:

Rnd 1: (K1, M1) around—124 (124, 124, 132, 132) sts.

Rnd 2: K1f&b around—248 (248, 248, 264, 264) sts. BO all sts loosely.

Sew in sleeves. Sew sleeve and side seams. Weave in ends. Block gently.

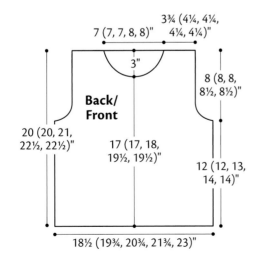

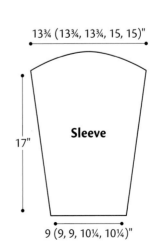

PINE TREE GUERNSEY

pine tree guernsey

Make this comfortable pullover in the Guernsey tradition, with richly patterned stitch work on top and plain stockinette stitch on the lower portion.

By Kerry Ferguson

Skill Level: Intermediate ◼◼◼◻

Sizes: S (M, L)

Finished Bust Measurement: 48 (50, 52)"

Finished Length: 27 (28, 29)"

materials

1700 (1800, 1900) yds of DK-weight 100% wool 〔3〕

Size 5 (3.75 mm) circular needle (29")

Size 7 (4.5 mm) circular needle (29") or size required to obtain gauge

Cable needle

6 stitch holders

4 stitch markers

5 buttons, approximately ⅝" diameter

gauge

20 sts and 26 rows = 4" in St st on larger needles

patterns

CABLED RIBBING

(Multiple of 5 sts + 5 sts)

Row 1 (RS): K2, P1, *K2, P1, K1, P1, rep from * 20 (21, 22) times more, ending K2.

Row 2: Knit the knit sts and purl the purl sts as they face you.

Row 3: K2, P1, *sk 1 st and knit into next st, knit into skipped st, sl both sts from needle tog, P1, K1, P1, rep from * 20 (21, 22) times more, ending K2.

Row 4: Knit the knit sts and purl the purl sts as they face you.

Rep rows 1–4.

PINE TREE PATTERN

(Worked over 55 sts)

C6B: Sl 3 sts to cn and hold at back, K3, K3 from cn.

C6F: Sl 3 sts to cn and hold at front, K3, K3 from cn.

Row 1 (RS): (P1, K1) 3 times, P1, K6, (P1, K1) 3 times, P1, K7, P1, K7, (P1, K1) 3 times, P1, K6, (P1, K1) 3 times, P1.

Row 2: K3, P1, K3, P6, K3, P1, K3, P6, K1, P1, K1, P6, K3, P1, K3, P6, K3, P1, K3.

Row 3: (P1, K1) 3 times, P1, K6, (P1, K1) 3 times, P1, K5, P1, K3, P1, K5, (P1, K1) 3 times, P1, K6, (P1, K1) 3 times, P1.

Row 4: K3, P1, K3, P6, K3, P1, K3, P4, K1, P2, K1, P2, K1, P4, K3, P1, K3, P6, K3, P1, K3.

Row 5: (P1, K1) 3 times, P1, C6B for left-hand side or C6F for right-hand side, (P1, K1) 3 times, P1, K3, P1, K2, P1, K1, P1, K2, P1, K3 (P1, K1) 3 times, P1, C6B or C6F, (P1, K1) 3 times, P1.

Row 6: K3, P1, K3, P6, K3, P1, K3, P2, K1, P2, K1, P3, K1, P2, K1, P2, K3, P1, K3, P6, K3, P1, K3.

Row 7: (P1, K1) 3 times, P1, K6, (P1, K1) 3 times, P1, K1, P1, K2, P1, K2, P1, K2, P1, K2, P1, K1, (P1, K1) 3 times, P1, K6, (P1, K1) 3 times, P1.

Row 8: K3, P1, K3, P6, K3, P1, K3, P3, K1, P2, K1, P1, K1, P2, K1, P3, K3, P1, K3, P6, K3, P1, K3.

Row 9: (P1, K1) 3 times, P1, K6, (P1, K1) 3 times, P1, K2, P1, K2, P1, K3, P1, K2, P1, K2, (P1, K1) 3 times, P1, K6, (P1, K1) 3 times, P1.

Row 10: K3, P1, K3, P6, K3, P1, K3, P4, K1, P2, K1, P2, K1, P4, K3, P1, K3, P6, K3, P1, K3.

Row 11: (P1, K1) 3 times, P1, C6B or C6F, (P1, K1) 3 times, P1, K3, P1, K2, P1, K1, P1, K2, P1, K3, (P1, K1) 3 times, P1, C6B or C6F, (P1, K1) 3 times, P1.

Row 12: K3, P1, K3, P6, K3, P1, K3, P5, K1, P3, K1, P5, K3, P1, K3, P6, K3, P1, K3.

Row 13: (P1, K1) 3 times, P1, K6, (P1, K1) 3 times, P1, K4, P1, K2, P1, K2, P1, K4, (P1, K1) 3 times, P1, K6, (P1, K1) 3 times, P1.

Row 14: K3, P1, K3, P6, K3, P1, K3, P6, K1, P1, K1, P6, K3, P1, K3, P6, K3, P1, K3.

Row 15: (P1, K1) 3 times, P1, K6, (P1, K1) 3 times, P1, K5, P1, K3, P1, K5, (P1, K1) 3 times, P1, K6, (P1, K1) 3 times, P1.

Row 16: K3, P1, K3, P6, K3, P1, K3, P7, K1, P7, K3, P1, K3, P6, K3, P1, K3.

Row 17: (P1, K1) 3 times, P1, C6B or C6F, (P1, K1) 3 times, P1, K6, P1, K1, P1, K6, (P1, K1) 3 times, P1, C6B or C6F, (P1, K1) 3 times, P1.

Row 18: K3, P1, K3, P6, K3, P1, K3, P15, K3, P1, K3, P6, K3, P1, K3.

Row 19: (P1, K1) 3 times, P1, K6, (P1, K1) 3 times, P1, K7, P1, K7, (P1, K1) 3 times, P1, K6, (P1, K1) 3 times, P1.

Row 20: K3, P1, K3, P6, K3, P1, K3, P15, K3, P1, K3, P6, K3, P1, K3.

Rep rows 1–20, crossing cables on every 6th row.

DOUBLE MOSS STITCH

(Multiple of 2 sts + 1 st)

Row 1: K1, *P1, K1, rep from * across.

Row 2: Knit the knit sts and purl the purl sts as they face you.

Row 3: P1, *K1, P1, rep from * across.

Row 4: Knit the knit sts and purl the purl sts as they face you.

Rep rows 1–4.

back

With smaller circular needle, CO 110 (114, 120) sts and work 6 reps (rows 1–4) of cabled ribbing. Inc 10 sts across last row of ribbing—120 (124, 130) sts.

Change to larger circular needle and work in St st. Work even until piece measures 14 (15, 16)" from beg, ending with RS row. Place st markers at each end of last row for armholes. Beg on WS row, knit 6 rows, inc 2 sts evenly across last row with M1 incs—122 (126, 132) sts. Fasten off yarn. Slide sts to opposite end of circular needle to start patt on RS row.

Join yarn and work patt as indicated for each size:

> **For S:** K3, work 55 sts in pine tree patt, work 6 sts in double moss st, work 55 sts in pine tree patt, K3.

> **For M:** K3, work 55 sts in pine tree patt, K2, work 6 sts in double moss st, K2, work 55 sts in pine tree patt, K3.

> **For L:** K2, P1, K1, P1, K1, work 55 sts in pine tree patt, K2, work 6 sts in double moss st, K2, work 55 sts in pine tree patt, K1, P1, K1, P1, K2.

Work even in est patts until pine tree patt has

been completed 3 times plus 18 rows more. Work across 43 (45, 48) sts, BO next 36 sts, join second ball of yarn and finish row. Working both sides at once and cont in patt, dec 1 st at neck edge every row twice—41 (43, 46) sts. When piece measures 12" from beg of 6 knit rows (garter band), place all sts on holders.

front

Work same as back until 6 rows of garter st (after placing markers for armholes) have been completed, with incs at each end of last row.

Work patt as indicated for each size:

> **For S:** K3, work 55 sts in pine tree patt, BO center 6 sts, attached second ball of yarn and work 55 sts in pine tree patt, K3.

> **For M:** K3, work 55 sts in pine tree patt, K2, BO center 6 sts, attach second ball of yarn and K2, work 55 sts in pine tree patt, K3.

> **For L:** K2, P1, K1, P1, K1, work 55 sts in pine tree patt, K2, BO center 6 sts, attach second ball of yarn and K2, work 55 sts in pine tree patt, K1, P1, K1, P1, K2.

Work both sides at once in est patt until pine tree patt has been completed 3 times plus 10 rows. On each side, place 12 center edge sts on holders. Cont in patt, dec 1 st at neck edge every other row 5 times. Work even until piece is same length as back. Place rem 41 (43, 46) sts on holders.

sleeves

With smaller circular needle, CO 44 sts. Work in cabled ribbing for 2½".

Change to larger circular needle and inc 16 sts across first row of St st—60 sts. Cont in St st, inc 1 st at each side of every third row 30 times—120 sts. Work even until sleeve measures 19" in total length. BO all sts very loosely with a needle 2 sizes larger.

finishing

Sew shoulder seams using 3-needle BO.

Collar: With RS facing you and smaller circular needle, work 12 sts in patt from holder; then PU 20 sts along side of neck, 47 sts across back of neck, 20 sts along other side of neck; work 12 sts from other holder—111 sts. Fasten off yarn. With RS facing you, join yarn and work in cabled ribbing as follows: K3, *K2, P1, K1, P1, rep from * 20 times, end K3. Work 12 rows of cabled ribbing. BO in patt.

Front placket: With RS facing you and smaller circular needle, PU sts along front edge, including neck, skipping approx every fifth st so that there are 46 sts on needle. Work 2 rows in K1, P1 ribbing, then work next row with buttonholes as follows: work 5 sts; *BO 2 sts, work 8 sts; rep from *; work 2 sts. On next row, cont in patt, working 2 backward loops (see page 126) over each bound-off st. Work even for 3 rows. BO. Work button side in same manner, but without buttonholes. Work 2 more rows. BO firmly. Sew on buttons.

Sew sleeves to body between markers. Sew sleeve and side seams. Weave in ends.

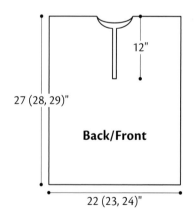

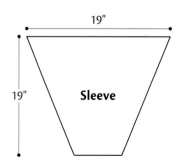

EASY MOHAIR PULLOVER

easy mohair pullover

Make it long or short—this is a great shape and easy as pie.

By Kerry Ferguson

Skill Level: Beginner ◖■□□▷

Sizes: S (M, L)

Finished Bust Measurement: 44 (46, 48)"

Finished Length:
   Short version: 19 (19, 21)"
   Long version: 24½ (25½, 25½)"

materials

Short version: 800 (800, 900) yds of bulky-weight mohair 🔢

Long version: 1000 (1000, 1100) yds of bulky-weight mohair 🔢

Size 8 (5 mm) needles

Size 8 (5 mm) circular needle (16") for neck

Size 10 (6 mm) needles or size required to obtain gauge

4 stitch holders

gauge

14 sts and 18 rows = 4" in St st on larger needles

back

With smaller needles, CO 76 (78, 86) sts. Work 4 rows in St st. Work in K2, P2 ribbing for 2".

Change to larger needles and work in St st. Work even until piece measures 10 (10, 11)" from beg for short version or 15½ (16½, 16½)" for long version.

Shape armholes: BO 3 sts at beg of next 2 rows. Dec 1 st at each end of EOR 4 times—62 (64, 72) sts.

Work even until piece measures 19 (19, 21)" from beg for short version, or 24½ (25½, 25½)" for long version. Place all sts on holder.

front

Work same as for back until piece measures 16 (16, 18)" from beg for short version, or 23 (24, 24)" for long version. Work across 22 (23, 27) sts, place next 18 sts on a holder, attach second ball of yarn and finish row. Working both sides at once, dec at neck edge 1 st EOR 3 times—19 (20, 24) sts each side. When piece measures same length as back, place rem sts on holders.

sleeves

With smaller needles, CO 28 (28, 32) sts. Work 4 rows in St st. Work in K2, P2 ribbing for 2".

Change to larger needles and work in St st, inc 1 st at each end of every third row 18 times—64 (64, 68) sts.

Work even until piece measures 17½ (17½, 18½)" from beg. BO 3 sts at beg of next 2 rows. Dec 1 st at each end of next 16 rows. BO rem 26 (26, 30) sts.

finishing

With RS tog, sew shoulder seams and BO back neck as follows: BO 19 (20, 24) sts using 3-needle BO (see page 127) for first shoulder, BO 24 sts in standard BO for back neck, BO 19 (20, 24) sts using 3-needle BO for second shoulder. Sew in sleeves. Sew underarm seams.

Collar: With small circular needle, and RS facing you, PU sts evenly around neck, join, pm, and work in K2, P2 ribbing for 2¼", then work 4 rows St st. BO loosely in ribbing.

Weave in ends.

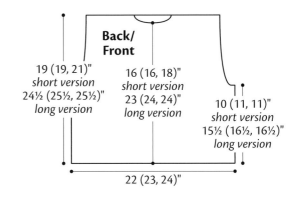

Back/Front

19 (19, 21)"
short version
24½ (25½, 25½)"
long version

16 (16, 18)"
short version
23 (24, 24)"
long version

10 (11, 11)"
short version
15½ (16½, 16½)"
long version

22 (23, 24)"

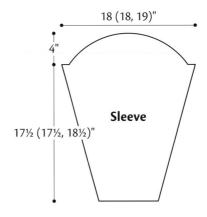

18 (18, 19)"

4"

Sleeve

17½ (17½, 18½)"

butterfly pullover

Intense stripes of color give lots of impact, while a butterfly band gives interest and playfulness to this garment. Two-color cuffs and collar pull this sweater together.

By Lori Ihnen

Skill Level: Intermediate ◖■■■◗

Sizes: S (M, L, 1X)

Finished Bust Measurement: 39 (42, 45, 48)"

Finished Length: 21½ (22¼, 23, 24)"

materials

Super fine-weight 100% wool (🧶1)

    720 (720, 900, 900) yds of red

    360 (360 (540, 540) yds of cinnamon

    360 (360 (540, 540) yds of fuchsia

    360 (360 (540, 540) yds of pink

    180 yds of raisin

    180 yds of dark plum

    180 yds of dark grape

    180 yds of green

Size 0 (2 mm) circular needle

Size 1 (2.5 mm) circular needle

Size 2 (3 mm) circular needle or size required to obtain gauge

1 stitch holder

1 stitch marker

gauge

30 sts and 36 rows = 4" in stranded knitting on larger needles

29 sts and 39 rows = 4" in plain St st on larger needles

back

With size 0 needle and cinnamon, CO 148 (158, 170, 182) sts; leave a long tail to sew hem later. Knit 10 rows even (1"), ending with a WS row.

Change to size 1 needle, *K2tog, YO*, rep from * to *, end K2tog (you will lose 1 st)—147 (157, 169, 181) sts. Knit 3 rows even, then change to red for 1 row.

Change to size 2 needle. Work all rows from chart on pages 86 and 87. On last row of chart (dark grape row), evenly dec 6 sts—141 (151, 163, 175) sts.

Work in stripe sequence below until piece measures 14 (14¼, 14½, 15)" from YO-K2tog row, ending with completed WS row.

Stripe sequence:

8 rows	red
1 row	cinnamon
5 rows	pink
3 rows	cinnamon
6 rows	fuchsia

Shape armholes: Cont in stripe sequence, at beg of each row, BO 3 sts 4 times, 2 sts 4 times, and 1 st

BUTTERFLY PULLOVER

6 (10, 10, 10) times—115 (121, 133 145) sts.

Work even until piece measures 20¾ (21½, 22¼, 23¼)" from YO-K2tog row, ending with a WS row.

Shape neck and shoulder: K37 (40, 44, 48) sts; attach second ball of yarn and BO center 41 (41, 45, 49) sts, finish row. Working both sides at once, at each neck edge, BO 5 sts once, then 3 sts once. Work 3 rows even. BO rem 29 (32, 36, 40) sts for each shoulder.

front

Work as for back (including armhole shaping) until piece measures 17½ (17¾, 18, 18¾)" from YO-K2tog row, ending with a WS row—115 (121, 133, 145) sts.

Shape neck and shoulder: K47 (50, 55, 60) sts, put center 21 (21, 23, 25) sts on holder, join second ball of yarn and finish row. Working both sides at once, at each neck edge, BO 4 sts once, 3 sts once, 2 sts twice, 1 st 3 times, then 1 st EOR 4 (4, 5, 6) times.

Work even until piece measures the same as back. BO rem 29 (32, 36, 40) sts for each shoulder.

sleeves

With size 2 needle and cinnamon, CO 71 (71, 75, 75) sts. Add red and work two-color ribbing as follows:

Row 1 (RS): *K3 with red, P1 with cinnamon*, rep from * to *, end K3 with red.

Row 2 (WS): Purl the purl sts, knit the knit sts as they face you, matching the colors as est.

Work two-color ribbing for 2 (2, 1¾, 1¾)".

Work in St st in stripe sequence as follows:

1 row	cinnamon
5 rows	pink
3 rows	cinnamon
6 rows	fuchsia
8 rows	red

AT SAME TIME, inc 1 st at each side every 8 (7, 6, 5) rows 19 (22, 24, 28) times—109 (115, 123, 131) sts. Work even until piece measures 20¼ (20¼, 20½, 20½)" from beg.

Shape cap: At each edge, BO 3 sts twice, 2 sts twice, 1 st 3 (5, 5, 5) times. BO rem 83 (85, 93, 101) sts.

finishing

Block pieces to measurements. Sew shoulders and side seams. Sew picot hem.

Neckband: With RS facing you, size 2 circular needle, and cinnamon, start at right back seam and PU 79 (79, 83, 87) sts across back, 30 (34, 39, 44) sts across right front, K21 (21, 23, 25) sts from holder, PU 30 (34, 39, 44) sts across left front—160 (168, 184, 200) sts. Join, pm, add red and work two-color ribbing as for sleeves. Cont in patt until neckband measures 1½". BO loosely with cinnamon.

Sew sleeve seams. Sew sleeves into armholes.

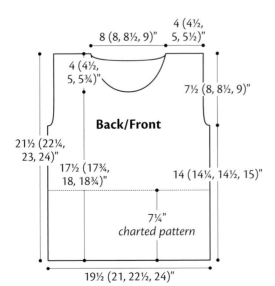

4 (4½, 5, 5½)"
8 (8, 8½, 9)"
4 (4½, 5, 5¾)"
7½ (8, 8½, 9)"
Back/Front
21½ (22¼, 23, 24)"
17½ (17¾, 18, 18¾)"
14 (14¼, 14½, 15)"
7¼"
charted pattern
19½ (21, 22½, 24)"

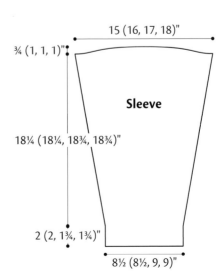

15 (16, 17, 18)"
¾ (1, 1, 1)"
Sleeve
18¼ (18¼, 18¾, 18¾)"
2 (2, 1¾, 1¾)"
8½ (8½, 9, 9)"

Color Key

Dark grape
Green
Dark plum
Red
Raisin
Cinnamon

S

M

L

1X

1 3 5 7 9 11 13 15 17 19 21 23 25 27 29 31 33 35 37 39 41 43 45 47 49 51 53 55 57 59

Pattern continues along this line.

VINE AND BIRDS PULLOVER

vine and birds pullover

This contoured-fit pullover features flowing vines and leaves, with birds nestled within. Garter-stitch edges provide a nice, crisp finish.

By Lori Ihnen

Skill Level: Intermediate ◼◼◼◻

Sizes: S (M, L, IX)

Finished Bust Measurement: 36 (38, 41, 44)"

Finished Length: 23 (24¾, 24½, 26½)"

materials

Super fine-weight 100% wool (1)

    1100 (1100, 1250, 1450) yds of dark blue

    900 (900, 1100, 1100) yds of light blue

Size 1 (2.5mm) circular needle

One set size 1 (2.5 mm) double-pointed needles

Size 2 (3 mm) circular needle or size required to obtain gauge

One set size 2 (3 mm) double-pointed needles

2 stitch markers

2 stitch holders

gauge

33 sts and 35¼ rows = 4" in stranded knitting on larger needle

body

The body is knit in the round to beg of armholes and then knit back and forth.

With size 1 needle and dark blue, CO 338 (354, 374, 398) sts. Work in garter st (knit 1 row, purl 1 row) for 1½".

Change to size 2 needle. Follow chart on pages 91 and 92 for color changes and shaping, pm at side seams. Place front and back center neck sts on holders.

sleeves

The sleeves are knit in the round until cap shaping, and then knit back and forth.

With size 1 dpns and dark blue, CO 70 (72, 74, 74) sts. Work in garter st for 1½".

Change to size 2 dpns. Follow chart on page 93 for color changes and shaping.

finishing

Sew shoulder seams.

Neckband: With RS facing you, size 1 dpns and dark blue, PU 11 sts on right back neck, K45 from back holder, PU 11 sts on left back neck, 23 sts across right front to holder, K25 from holder, PU 23 sts across left front—138 sts. Work in garter st for 1". BO loosely.

Block pieces to measurements. Sew sleeves to body. Weave in ends.

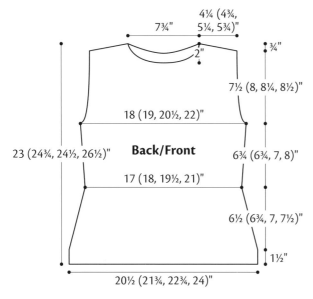

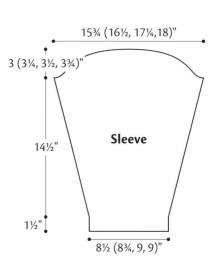

Back/Front

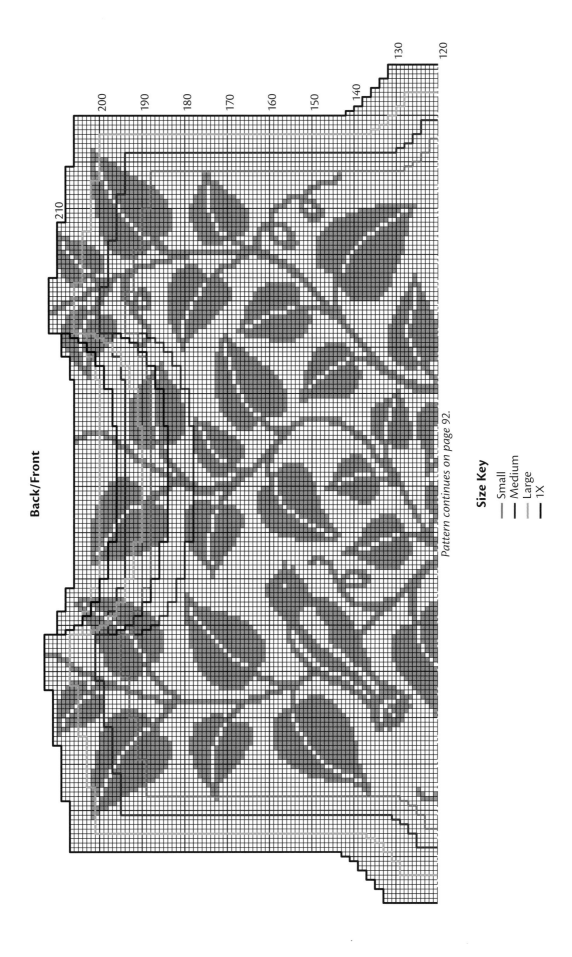

Pattern continues on page 92.

Size Key
— Small
— Medium
— Large
— 1X

Pattern continues on page 91.

VINE AND BIRDS PULLOVER

Sleeve

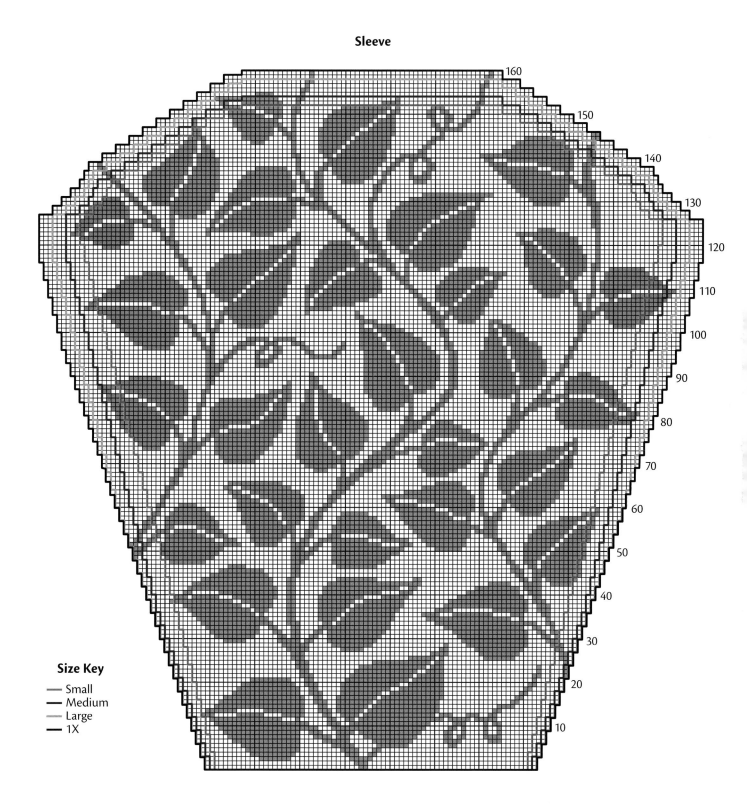

160
150
140
130
120
110
100
90
80
70
60
50
40
30
20
10

Size Key
— Small
— Medium
— Large
— 1X

CARDIGANS AND JACKETS

rose blossom cardigan

Luxurious soft alpaca in a flattering silhouette is shaped by changing needle sizes. Three-dimensional flowers adorn the bell-shaped sleeves.

By Lori Ihnen

Skill Level: Easy ■■□□

Sizes: Petite (S, M, L)

Finished Bust Measurement: 36 (38, 40, 44)"

Finished Length: 17 (18, 18¾, 20¼)"

materials

1300 (1550, 1775, 2100) yds of sport-weight 100% alpaca **2**

Very small amounts of fingering-weight cotton in red, burgundy, and green (for flowers) **1**

Size 1 (2.5 mm) circular needle

Size 2 (3 mm) circular needle or size required to obtain gauge

Size 3 (3.25 mm) circular needle

Size 4 (3.5 mm) straight needles

2 stitch holders

7 (7, 7, 8) stitch markers

6 (6, 6, 7) buttons, ⅝" diameter

gauge

Unblocked: 44 sts and 35 rows = 4" in rib stitch on size 2 needle

Blocked: 40 sts and 34 rows = 4" in rib stitch on size 2 needle

Note that alpaca yarn has a tendency to grow in length; also, because the body is knit with a rib stitch, it can grow in width. If trying to decide between sizes, go with the smaller size, as it will grow easily or can be blocked larger with ease.

rib stitch

Row 1 (RS): *P3, K2; rep from * to last 3 sts, end P3.

All other rows: Knit the knit sts and purl the purl sts as they face you.

body

The body is worked in one piece to beg of armholes.

With size 3 needle and alpaca, CO 358 (378, 398, 438) sts. Work in rib st for 4 (4, 4½, 4¾)".

Change to size 2 needle. Cont in est patt until piece measures 9¾ (10½, 10¾, 11)", ending with a WS row.

Shape armholes and divide for back and fronts: Work as est across 84 (89, 94, 104) sts and place on holder, BO 10 sts, K170 (180, 190, 210) sts, BO 10 sts, work across rem 84 (89, 94, 104) sts and place on holder. Working on back only, attach new yarn, BO 2 sts at beg of next 2 (2, 6, 10) rows, and 1 st at beg of next 12 (12, 8, 4) rows—154 (164, 170, 186) sts. Work even until armhole measures 7¼ (7½, 8, 9¼)", ending with completed WS row.

Shape back neck and shoulder: BO 12 (12, 13, 14) sts, work across 48 (50, 52, 56) sts, BO center 34 (40, 40, 46) sts, finish row. Turn and work this side first: At side edge, BO 12 (12, 13, 14) sts once, 11 (12, 13, 14) sts once, 11 (12, 12, 14) sts once, and 11 (11, 12, 13) sts once; AT SAME TIME at neck edge, BO 6 sts once, 5 sts once, and 4 sts once. On WS, attach yarn at neck edge and work opposite side as follows: At neck edge, BO 6 sts once, 5 sts once, and 4 sts once; AT SAME TIME, at side edge BO 11 (12, 13, 14) sts once, 11 (12, 12, 14) sts once, and 11 (11, 12, 13) sts once.

left front

At armhole edge, BO 2 sts 1 (1, 3, 5) times, then BO 1 st 6 (6, 4, 2) times—76 (81, 84, 92) sts. Work even until piece measures 12½ (13½, 14¼, 15¾)", ending with RS row.

Shape neck: At neck edge, BO 2 sts 11 (13, 13, 16) times, then BO 1 st 9 (8, 8, 5) times—45 (47, 50, 55) sts. Work even until same length as back to shoulder, then shape shoulder as for back.

right front

Work as for left front, reversing shaping.

sleeves

With size 3 needle and alpaca, CO 68 (73, 78, 83) sts. Work in rib st for 1".

Change to size 2 needle, work as est for 2" more, ending with completed WS row.

Dec row: K2, *K2tog, ssk, K1; rep from * to last st, end K1—42 (45, 48, 51) sts.

Change to size 4 needles, work in St st, and inc 1 st at each side every 5 (5, 5, 4) rows 19 (19, 20, 25) times—80 (83, 88, 101) sts.

Work even until piece measures 19¼ (19½, 20, 20½)", ending with a WS row.

Shape cap: BO 5 sts at beg of next 2 rows, 2 sts at beg of next 2 (2, 6, 10) rows, and 1 st at beg of next 12 (12, 8, 4) rows. BO rem 54 (57, 58, 67) sts.

finishing

Block pieces to measurements. Sew shoulder seams.

Neckbands: With size 1 needle and alpaca, PU 100 (108, 114, 126) sts at beg of lower right front, pm, PU 45 (46, 46, 47) sts along right V-neck, 52 (56, 56, 60) sts across back, 45 (46, 46, 47) sts along left V-neck, and 100 (108, 114, 120) sts along left front—342 (364, 376, 400) sts. Pm for 6 (6, 6, 7) buttons on left front, starting ½" down from marker and ½" up from bottom.

Rows 1–6: Work K1, P1 ribbing; on row 3 of right front, work buttonholes opposite markers as follows: BO 2 sts for each buttonhole; on return row, CO 2 sts. BO in patt.

Sew sleeve seams. Sew sleeves into armholes. Sew on buttons.

Leaves (Make 4): On rows 3 and 7, knit into back of YO sts. With size 3 needle and green, make slipknot, K1, and place on needle—2 sts.

Row 1: K2.

Row 2: K1, YO, K1.

Rows 3, 4, and 5: K3.

Row 6: K1, YO, K1, YO, K1.

Rows 7, 8, 9, 10, and 11: K5.

Row 12: Ssk, K1, K2tog.

Row 13: K3.

Row 14: Sl 2 sts tog as if to knit, K1, P2sso.

Cut yarn and pull loop through. To identify RS, note that WS has slants where YOs were knit into back. Use tails to sew down, two leaves per flower.

Weave in ends.

Flowers (make 2 red and 2 burgundy): With size 3 needle, cable CO 30 sts; leave tail long enough to attach flowers later. K3, *(turn, K3) 5 times, turn, BO 3 sts, K2*, rep from * to *. On last petal after BO, pull CO tail through last bound-off loop to finish off. Use tails to attach to body. Note that flower naturally wants to coil inward; sew it down the opposite of its natural coil and the flower will lie open more. Coil 1 red flower and 1 burgundy flower tog; attach to cuffs.

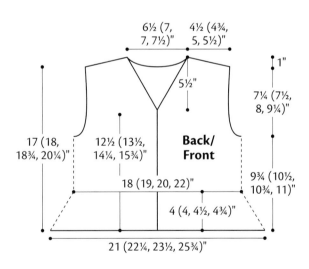

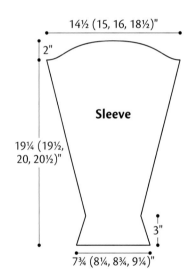

aran cardigan

Step into the stream of history as you create your Aran cardigan. You will be knitting it in the same way the Aran islanders have done it for centuries, from the top down. Don't be afraid to try a favorite stitch that will make it your very own.

By Kerry Ferguson

Skill Level: Intermediate ▰▰▰▱

Sizes: S (M, L)

Finished Bust Measurement: 48 (50, 52)"

Finished Length:
  Short version: 21 (22, 23)"
  Long version: 28 (29, 31)"

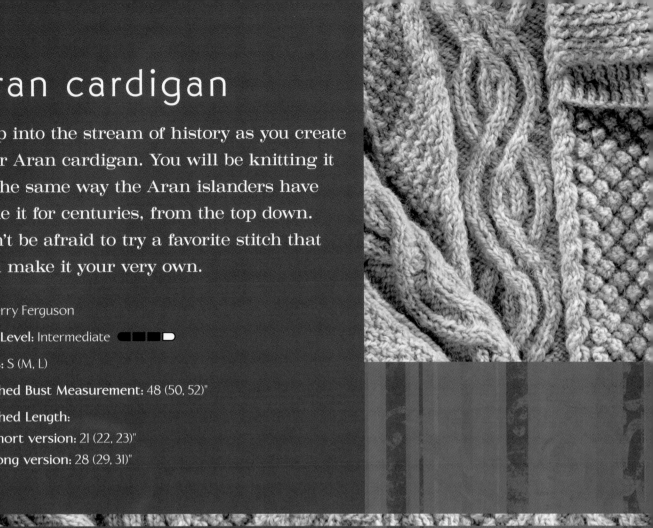

materials

Worsted-weight 100% wool **(4)**
  Short version: 1290 (1440, 1600) yds
  Long version: 1600 (1760, 2080) yds

Size 6 (4.25 mm)

Size 8 (5 mm) circular needle or size to obtain correct gauge

Cable needle

4 stitch holders

7 (10 for long version) buttons, 1" diameter

gauge

18 sts and 22 rows = 4" in double moss st on larger needles

(Composite gauge of varied sts will be different, but if double moss is correct, the garment size will be correct.)

patterns

DOUBLE MOSS STITCH
(Multiple of 2 sts)

Row 1 (RS): *K1, P1; rep from * across.

Row 2: Knit the knit sts, and purl the purl sts as they face you.

Row 3: *P1, K1; rep from * across.

Row 4: Knit the knit sts, and purl the purl sts as they face you.

Rep rows 1–4.

TRIPLE CROSS

(Multiple of 3 sts)

Row 1 (RS): K3.

Row 2: P3.

Row 3: Sk first st, K2, then knit first st.

Row 4: P3.

Rep rows 1–4.

DOUBLE WAVE CABLE (chart on page 103)

(Worked over 16 sts)

C4B: Sl 2 sts to cn and hold at back, K2, K2 from cn.

C4F: Sl 2 sts to cn and hold at front, K2, K2 from cn.

T3B: Sl 1 st to cn and hold at back, K2, P1 from cn.

T3F: Sl 2 sts to cn and hold at front, P1, K2 from cn.

Row 1 (RS): K2, P3, K2, P2, K2, P3, K2.

Row 2 and all even-numbered rows: Knit the knit sts, and purl the purl sts as they face you.

Row 3: T3F, P2, T3F; T3B, P2, T3B.

Row 5: P1, T3F; P2; C4F, P2, T3B, P1.

Row 7: P2, (T3F, T3B) twice, P2.

Row 9: P3, C4F, P2, C4F, P3.

Row 11: P2, (T3B, T3F) twice, P2.

Row 13: P1, T3B, P2, C4F, P2, T3F, P1.

Row 15: T3B, P2, T3B, T3F, P2, T3F.

Row 16: Rep Row 2.

Rows 17–32: Rep Rows 1–16, but work C4B instead of C4F on 5th, 9th, and 13th rows.

Rep rows 1–32.

TRINITY STITCH (chart on page 104)

(Multiple of 4 sts + 2 sts)

Row 1 (RS): Purl.

Row 2: K1; *(K1, P1, K1) in same st, P3tog; rep from * to last st; K1.

Row 3: Purl.

Row 4: K1; *P3tog, (K1, P1, K1) in same st; rep from * to last st; K1.

Rep rows 1–4.

RIGHT ARAN HALF-DIAMOND (chart on page 105)

(Worked over 7 sts)

Row A (worked only once): P5, K2

Row 1 (WS): P2, K5.

Row 2 (RS): P4, T3B.

Row 3 and all odd rows: Knit the knit sts, and purl the purl sts as they face you.

Row 4: P3, T3B, K1.

Row 6: P2, T3B, K1, P1.

Row 8: P1, T3B, K1, P1, K1.

Row 10: T3B, (K1, P1) twice.

Row 12: T3F, (P1, K1) twice.

Row 14: P1, T3F, P1, K1, P1.

Row 16: P2, T3F, P1, K1.

Row 18: P3, T3F, P1.

Row 20: P4, T3F.

Rep rows 1–20.

LEFT ARAN HALF-DIAMOND (chart on page 105)

(Worked over 7 sts)

Row A (worked only once): K2, P5.

Row 1 (WS): K5, P2.

Row 2: T3F, P4.

Row 3 and all odd rows: Knit the knit sts, and purl the purl sts as they face you.

Row 4: K1, T3F, P3.

Row 6: P1, K1, T3F, P2.

Row 8: K1, P1, K1, T3F, P1.

Row 10: (P1, K1) twice, T3F.

Row 12: (K1, P1) twice, T3B.

Row 14: P1, K1, P1, T3B, P1.

Row 16: K1, P1, T3B, P2.

Row 18: P1, T3B, P3.

Row 20: T3B, P4.

Rep rows 1–20.

ARAN DIAMOND WITH MOSS STITCH
(chart on page 104)
(Worked over 13 sts)

BC (Back Cross): Sl 1 st to cn and hold in back, K1tbl, P1 from cn.

FC (Front Cross): Sl 1 st to cn and hold in front, P1, K1tbl from cn.

Row 1 (RS): P5, sl next 2 sts to cn and hold in front, K1tbl, then sl 1 purl st from cn to left-hand needle and purl it, K1tbl from cn, P5.

Row 2: K5, P1, K1, P1, K5.

Row 3: P4, BC, K1, FC, P4.

Row 4 and all other even rows: Knit the knit sts, and purl the purl sts as they face you.

Row 5: P3, BC, K1, P1, K1, FC, P3.

Row 7: P2, BC, (K1, P1) twice, K1, FC, P2.

Row 9: P1, BC, (K1, P1) 3 times, K1, FC, P1.

Row 11: BC, (K1, P1) 4 times, K1, FC.

Row 13: FC, (P1, K1) 4 times, P1, BC.

Row 15: P1, FC, (P1, K1) 3 times, P1, BC, P1.

Row 17: P2, FC, (P1, K1) twice, P1, BC, P2.

Row 19: P3, FC, P1, K1, P1, BC, P3.

Row 21: P4, FC, P1, BC, P4.

Row 22: Rep row 2.

Rep rows 1–22.

neck and saddle shoulders

With smaller needles, CO 99 sts. Work in K1tbl, P1 ribbing for 6" for collar. Place 10 sts on a holder; leave next 30 sts on needle; place rem 59 sts on a holder.

Change to larger circular needle and work 30 sts on needle as follows: K2, P2, K1tbl, P2, work 16 sts in double wave cable, P2, K1tbl, P2, K2. Work sts on either side of cable as they face you. Cont in est patt until piece measures 10 (10½, 11)" long from ribbing. Place sts on a holder.

Return to stitch holder with 59 sts. Place 19 sts for back on a holder, 30 sts on needles, and 10 sts on a holder. Work 30 sts on needles in same manner as other shoulder. Fasten off.

left front

With RS facing you, PU 10 neck sts from holder. Working along the saddle shoulder edge, PU 51 (53, 55) sts between the first row of edge sts and the next row. Fasten off so first row can be a RS row.

Set up patt as follows: K2, work 7 sts in left Aran half-diamond, work 3 sts in triple cross, work 14 sts in trinity st, work 3 sts in triple cross, P2, work 16 sts in double wave cable, P2, work 3 sts in triple cross, work 7 (9, 11) sts in double moss st, K2.

Cont in est patts until piece measures 8½" long from pick-up row. Place sts on a holder.

right front

Work right front in same manner as left front, reversing sequence and using Right Aran Half-Diamond.

back

With RS facing you, PU 117 (121, 125) sts, including 19 sts from holder. Fasten off yarn. Slide sts to opposite end of circular needle, join yarn and work first row of patt (RS row) as follows: K2, work 7 (9, 11) sts in double moss st, work 3 sts in triple cross, P2, work 16 sts in double wave cable, P2, work 3 sts in triple cross, work 14 sts in trinity st, work 3 sts in triple cross, work 13 sts in Aran diamonds with moss st, work 3 sts in triple cross, work 14 sts in trinity st, work 3 sts in triple cross, P2, work 16 sts in double wave cable, P2, work 3 sts in triple cross, work 7 (9, 11) sts in double moss st, K2.

Cont in est patts until back measures same length as fronts.

sleeves

Beg at underarm with RS facing you and larger needles, PU 38 sts along armhole edge, working between first and second st and skipping approx every fifth st. Work across sts on holder in patt. PU 38 sts on back armhole edge, again skipping approx every fifth st. Work in rnds or flat. Working sts on either side of shoulder cable in double moss st and cont est saddle shoulder patt, work even for 3".

Cont in patt, dec on either side of an imaginary underarm seam every fourth row until sleeve measures 14" from beg; work decs as follows: K1, ssk, work to last 3 sts, K2tog, K1. Dec to 46 sts across next row.

Change to smaller needles. Work in K1tbl, P1 ribbing, alternating with rounds of K1, P1tbl if working in the rnd, for 3". BO in ribbing.

completing fronts and backs

Place fronts and back tog on one needle. Cont in est patt, but knit the 2 edge sts tog at each armhole to make a panel of triple cross, inc between the 2 sts to make 3 for patt. Cont until length for pocket is reached, 16" from center of saddle shoulder for short version, 18" for long version. End ready for a RS row. Work 29 (31, 33) sts; work 20 sts and place on a holder; work to last 49 (51, 53) sts; work 20 sts and place on a holder; work 29 (31, 33) sts. On next row, CO 20 sts across each holder and cont in patt until piece measures 19 (20, 21)" from center of saddle shoulder for short version, 25 (26, 28)" for long version.

Change to smaller needles and work in K1tbl, P1 ribbing for 2" (short version) or 3" (long version). BO in ribbing.

finishing

Front bands: With RS facing you and smaller needles, PU sts along left front edge, skipping approx every fifth st. Work in K1tbl, P1 ribbing for 2 rows. In next row, work 7 buttonholes for short version, or 10 buttonholes for long version, placing one 1" from bottom, then approx 3" apart, ending with one 1" from top. **Make buttonholes as follows:** Work to buttonhole; *BO 2 sts, CO 2 sts over them with a simple backward loop cast-on (see page 126), cont to next buttonhole; rep from * until all buttonholes are made. Work 2 more rows, then BO firmly. Work other band in same manner, but without buttonholes. Sew on buttons.

Pockets: Pick up pocket sts from holders and work 3½" of pocket lining in patt. BO in patt. Tack down. PU cast-on sts and work 5 rows of K1tbl, P1 ribbing. BO in ribbing. Tack down.

Weave in ends.

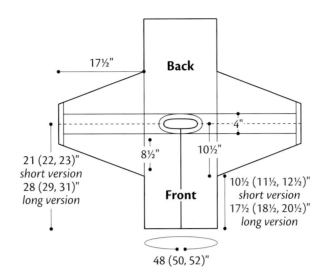

Back

17½"

4"

8½"

10½"

21 (22, 23)"
short version
28 (29, 31)"
long version

Front

10½ (11½, 12½)"
short version
17½ (18½, 20½)"
long version

48 (50, 52)"

Double Wave Cable

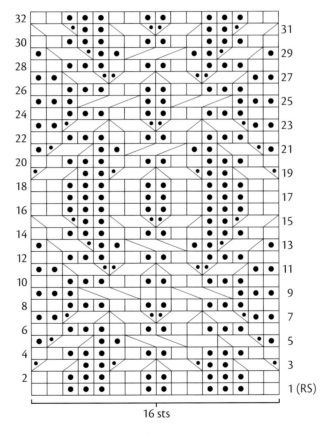

16 sts

Key

☐ K on RS, P on WS

● P on RS, K on WS

T3B: Sl 1 st to cn and hold at front, K2, P1 from cn.

T3F: Sl 2 sts to cn and hold at front, P1, K2 from cn.

C4B: Sl 2 sts to cn and hold at back, K2, K2 from cn.

C4F: Sl 2 sts to cn and hold at front, K2, K2 from cn.

Trinity Stitch

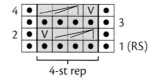

4-st rep

Key

●	K on WS, P on RS
V	K1, P1, K1 in same st
⟍	P3tog

Aran Diamond with Moss Stitch

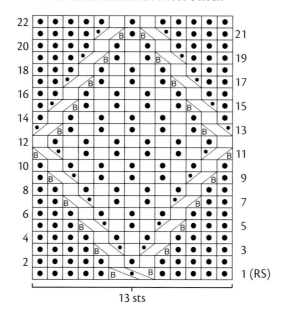

13 sts

Key

☐	K on RS, P on WS
●	P on RS, K on WS
▨	BC: Sl 1 st to cn and hold at back, K1tbl, P1 from cn.
▨	FC: Sl 1 st to cn and hold at front, P1, K1tbl from cn.
▨	Sl 2 sts to cn and hold at front, K1tbl, sl 1 purl st from cn to left-hand needle and purl it, K1tbl from cn.

Right Aran Half-Diamond

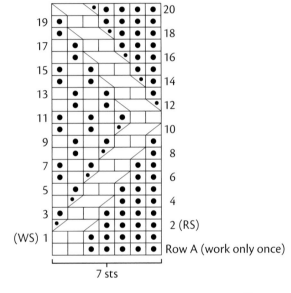

7 sts

Left Aran Half-Diamond

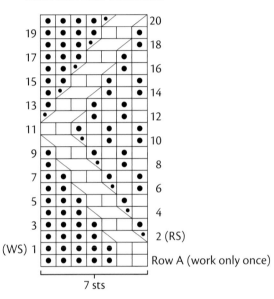

7 sts

Key

☐ K on RS, P on WS

● P on RS, K on WS

T3B: Sl 1 st to cn and hold at front, K2, P1 from cn.

T3F: Sl 2 sts to cn and hold at front, P1, K2 from cn.

TRADITIONAL FLORAL CARDIGAN

traditional floral cardigan

Traditional shaping and a simple pattern repeat make this relaxed cardigan a fun one to make. A colorful lower band and picot edging finish off the garment.

By Lori Ihnen

Skill Level: Intermediate ⬤⬤⬤◻

Sizes: S (M, L, IX)

Finished Bust Measurement: 38 (42, 45, 48)"

Finished Length: 23 (23½, 23½, 24)"

materials

Super fine-weight 100% wool

    1260 (1440, 1440, 1620) yds of red

    720 (720, 900, 900) yds of white

    180 (360, 360, 360) yards of blue

    180 yds of dark green

    180 yds of light green

    180 yds of gold

Size 1 (2.5 mm) circular needle or size required to obtain gauge

Size 2 (3 mm) circular needle

4 stitch markers

2 stitch holders

7 buttons, ¾" diameter

gauge

30 sts and 36 rows = 4" in stranded knitting on larger needle

body

The body is knit in one piece to beg of armholes.

With smaller needle and red, CO 286 (310, 334, 358) sts. Knit 6 rows in St st.

Change to larger needle. **Picot edge (RS):** *YO, K2tog, rep from * to end. **Next row:** YO, purl to end. You will gain 1 st.

Beg row 1 of chart on page 111 and pm as follows: K71 (77, 83, 89) sts, pm, K1, pm, K143 (155, 167, 179) sts, pm, K1, pm, K71 (77, 83, 89) sts. The st between markers is center underarm st. Follow front and back chart for color and shaping to beg of armhole.

Shape armholes and divide for back and fronts: Cont in patt, K69 (75, 81, 87) sts and place on holder. BO 5 sts, K139 (151, 163, 175) sts, BO 5 sts, K69 (75, 81, 87) sts and place on holder.

Working back and forth, follow back chart for color and shaping.

left front

Pick up sts for left front and follow left front chart for color and shaping. BO sts or place on holder for 3-needle BO.

right front

Pick up sts for right front and follow right front chart for color and shaping. BO sts or place on holder for 3-needle BO.

sleeves

With smaller needle and red, CO 59 (63, 63, 67) sts. Work in K1, P1 ribbing for 1½".

Change to larger needle. Working from sleeve chart on page 110, inc 1 st at each side EOR 6 (7, 7, 8) times and 1 st at each side every 5 rows 28 (29, 29, 30) times—127 (135, 135, 143) sts.

Work even until sleeve measures 21 (21¼, 21¼, 21¼)".

Shape cap: BO 2 sts at beg of next 12 rows, then 1 st at beg of next 2 rows. BO rem 101 (109, 109, 117) sts.

finishing

Block pieces to measurements.

Sew or work 3-needle BO to join shoulders. Fold picot edge at YO row and sew hem in place.

Collar: With smaller needle and red, PU 36 (38, 38, 40) sts on right front, 47 (49, 49, 51) sts across back, 36 (38, 38, 40) sts on left front—119 (125, 125, 131) sts. Work in K1, P1 ribbing for 1". BO in patt.

Button band: With RS facing you, smaller needle and red, PU 155 (159, 159, 163) sts on left front. Work in K1, P1 ribbing for 1". BO in patt.

Buttonhole band: Work as for button band, making 7 buttonholes evenly spaced ½" from PU row, with the first and last buttonholes 1" from top and bottom edges. BO 3 sts for each buttonhole and CO 3 sts on return row.

Sew sleeve seams. Set sleeves into armholes. Sew on buttons. Weave in ends.

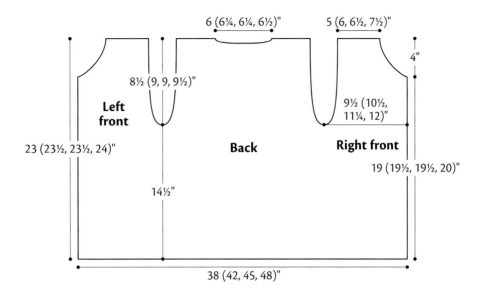

6 (6¼, 6¼, 6½)"

5 (6, 6½, 7½)"

4"

8½ (9, 9, 9½)"

Left front

9½ (10½, 11¼, 12)"

23 (23½, 23½, 24)"

Back

Right front

19 (19½, 19½, 20)"

14½"

38 (42, 45, 48)"

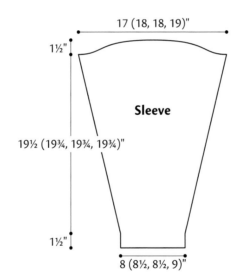

17 (18, 18, 19)"

1½"

Sleeve

19½ (19¾, 19¾, 19¾)"

1½"

8 (8½, 8½, 9)"

Sleeve

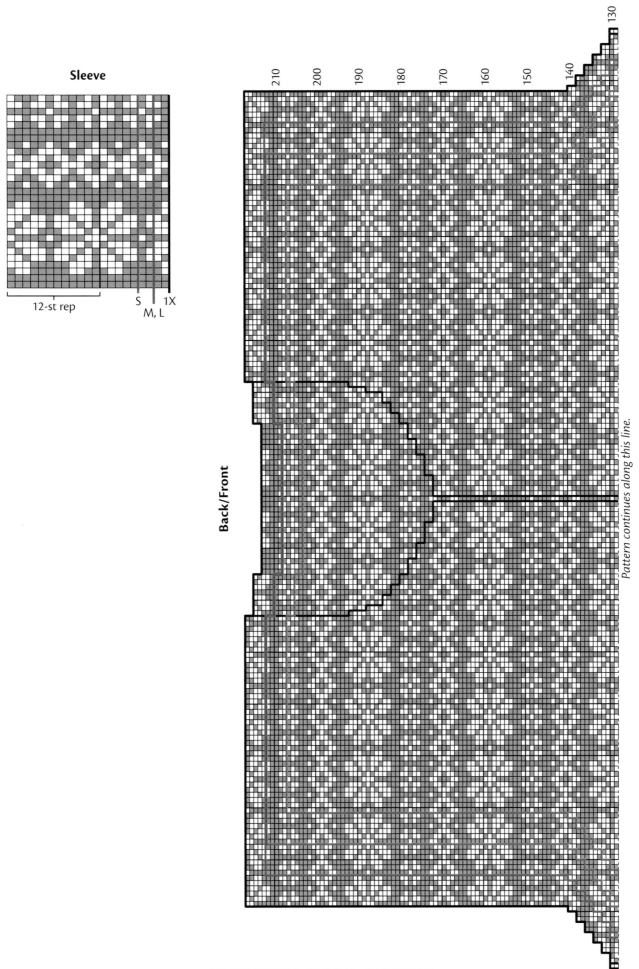

12-st rep

S   1X
M, L

Back/Front

210 200 190 180 170 160 150 140 130

Pattern continues along this line.

   TRADITIONAL FLORAL CARDIGAN

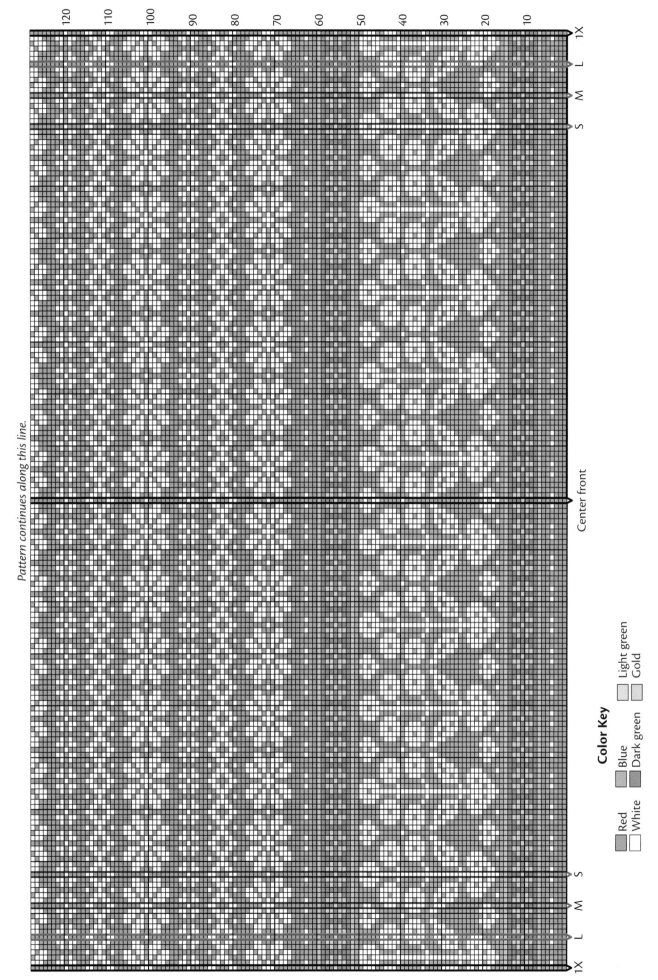

Pattern continues along this line.

Center front

120 110 100 90 80 70 60 50 40 30 20 10

1X L M S

S M L 1X

Color Key

Red		Blue	Light green
White		Dark green	Gold

Cont in St st until piece measures 13 (14, 16, 17, 17)" from beg.

Shape neck: At neck edge, work dec as follows: (K4, ssk, knit to end) EOR 6 times. Place 4 sts at neck edge on holder. BO 4 sts at neck edge, dec 1 st at neck edge EOR 3 times—9 (11, 12, 14, 15) sts.

Cont in St st until piece measures 19 (20, 22, 23, 23)" from beg. BO rem sts. Mark position for 4 buttons along center front edge, starting 1½" from bottom edge and ending 1" from top.

right front

Work as for left front, reversing shaping and working armhole dec as follows: Knit to last 4 sts, K2tog, K2. At same time, work 4 buttonholes to correspond with markers on left front, working buttonholes as follows: K2, YO, K2tog.

sleeves

CO 26 (26, 26, 26, 28) sts, work in garter st for 6 rows, inc 2 (2, 6, 6, 8) sts evenly across last row—28 (28, 32, 32, 36) sts.

Work in St st, inc 1 st at each edge every 6 rows 8 times—44 (44, 48, 48, 52). For better seams, work inc 2 sts from edge.

Cont in St st until 15 (16, 16½, 16½, 17)" or desired length from beg.

Shape cap: BO 3 sts at beg of next 2 rows. Work dec row as follows: (K2, ssk, knit to last 4 sts, K2tog, K2) EOR 11 times, BO 2 sts at beg of next 4 rows—8 (8, 12, 12, 16) sts. BO rem sts.

finishing

Sew shoulder seams.

Neckband: With RS facing you, knit 4 sts from holder, PU 46 sts along neck edge, and knit 4 sts from holder—54 sts. Work in garter st for 5 rows. BO all sts loosely.

Sew in sleeves. Sew sleeve and side seams. Sew on buttons to correspond with buttonholes. Weave in ends.

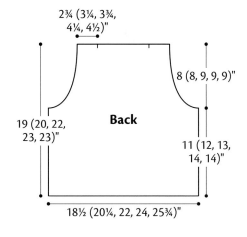

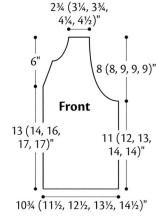

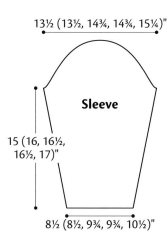

fake cable cardigan

Rich diagonal latticework creates a resilient dimension. A retro collar and buttons enhance the simple classic design.

By Melissa Matthay and Sheryl Thies

Skill Level: Intermediate

Sizes: S (M, L, 1X)

Finished Bust Measurement: 38¾ (42¾, 47¼, 53¼)"

Finished Length: 20½ (22, 24, 24)"

materials

1600 (1675, 1750, 1850) yds of worsted-weight 100% merino wool **4**

Size 5 (3.75 mm) needles

Size 8 (5 mm) needles or size required to obtain gauge

5 buttons, 1" diameter

gauge

24 sts and 24 rows = 4" in fake cable patt, slightly stretched, on larger needles

fake cable pattern

(Multiple of 9 sts + 2 sts)

C2L: Sk first st on left-hand needle, knit in back of second st, twist right-hand needle and sl front st as if to knit, slipping both sts off left-hand needle.

Row 1: *P2, C2L, K5, rep from *, end P2.

Row 2 and all even rows: *K2, P7, rep from *, end K2.

Row 3: *P2, K1, C2L, K4, rep from *, end P2.

Row 5: *P2, K2, C2L, K3, rep from *, end P2.

Row 7: *P2, K3, C2L, K2, rep from *, end P2.

Row 9: *P2, K4, C2L, K1, rep from *, end P2.

Row 11: *P2, K5, C2L, rep from *, end P2.

Row 12: *K2, P7, rep from *, end K2.

Rep rows 1–12.

back

With smaller needles, CO 119 (128, 137, 155) sts. Work in K1, P1 ribbing for 1½".

Change to larger needles, work fake cable patt until piece measures 12 (13½, 15½, 15½)" from beg.

Shape armholes: BO 3 sts at beg of next 2 rows, BO 2 sts at beg of next 2 rows, dec 1 st at each edge EOR 4 (4, 8, 13) times—101 (110, 111, 119) sts.

Cont in patt until piece measures 20½ (22, 24, 24)" from beg, BO rem sts in patt.

FAKE CABLE CARDIGAN

right front

With smaller needles, CO 56 (65, 74, 83) sts. Work as for back until piece measures 12 (13½, 15½, 15½)" from beg.

Shape armhole: BO 3 sts at side edge once, BO 2 sts at side edge once, dec 1 st at side edge 4 (4, 8, 13) times—47 (56, 61, 65) sts.

Cont in patt until piece measures 17½ (19, 21, 21)" from beg.

Shape neck: BO 5 (9, 12, 12) sts at neck edge once, BO 4 (5, 5, 5) sts at neck edge once, BO 3 (3, 4, 4) sts at neck edge once, BO 2 sts at neck edge once, dec 1 st at neck edge EOR 4 times—29 (33, 34, 38) sts.

Cont in patt until piece measures 20½ (22, 24, 24)" from beg. BO rem sts in patt.

left front

Work as for right front, reversing shaping.

sleeves

With smaller needles, CO 52 (60, 60, 60) sts. Work in K1, P1 ribbing for 1½", inc 13 (14, 14, 14) sts evenly across last row—65 (74, 74, 74) sts.

Change to larger needles, work fake cable patt, inc 1 st at each edge every 4 rows 24 times—113 (122, 122, 122) sts.

Cont in patt until piece measures 18" or desired length.

Shape cap: BO 4 sts at beg of next 2 rows, BO 3 sts at beg of next 2 rows, BO 2 sts at beg of next 2 rows, dec 1 st at each edge EOR 6 times. BO rem sts in patt.

finishing

Sew shoulder seams.

Right front band: With smaller needles and RS facing you, PU 68 (74, 78, 78) sts along right front edge and work in K1, P1 ribbing for 1¼", working 5 buttonholes into band as YO, K2tog about ⅝" from PU row. BO all sts in patt.

Left front band: Work as for right front band omitting buttonholes.

Collar: With smaller needles and WS facing you, PU 33 (37, 38, 42) sts along front neck, 43 (44, 43, 43) along back neck, 33 (37, 38, 42) sts along front neck—109 (118, 119, 127) sts. Work in K1, P1 ribbing for 3½". BO all sts in patt.

Sew in sleeves. Sew sleeve and side seams. Sew buttons on left front band to match buttonholes. Weave in ends.

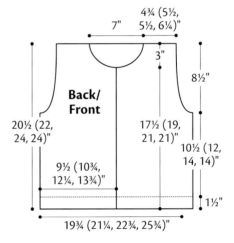

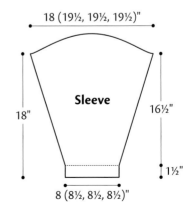

GRAPE SEED JACKET

grape seed jacket

This beautifully textured, versatile jacket features patch pockets and pointed collar.

By Melissa Matthay and Sheryl Thies

Skill Level: Easy ◖■■□▷

Sizes: XS (S, M, L, 1X)

Finished Bust Measurement: 40 (41½, 45, 48, 50½)"

Finished Length: 23 (24, 25, 26, 26)"

materials

800 (875, 950, 1025, 1100) yds of bulky-weight 100% wool (**5**)

Size 11 (8 mm) straight and circular needle, 24", or size required to obtain gauge

5 buttons, ⅞" diameter

gauge

12 sts and 16 rows = 4" in seed stitch

seed stitch

(Even number of sts)

Row 1: *K1, P1, rep from * across.

Row 2: *P1, K1; rep from * across. (Knit the purl sts and purl the knit sts as they face you.)

Rep rows 1 and 2.

back

CO 60 (64, 68, 72, 76) sts and work in seed st until piece measures 15 (16, 17, 17, 17)" from beg.

Shape armholes: BO 3 sts at beg of next 2 rows, dec 1 st at each edge EOR 3 (4, 5, 6, 7) times as follows: K1, ssk, work in patt to last 3 sts, K2tog, K1—48 (50, 52, 54, 56) sts.

Cont until piece measures 23 (24, 25, 26, 26)" from beg. BO all sts in patt.

right front

CO 36 (38, 40, 42, 44) sts and work in seed st until piece measures 14" from beg, ending with WS row.

Work buttonhole: On center edge, work in patt 3 sts, YO, K2tog, cont in patt across row. Rep buttonhole every 10 rows 4 more times. Cont until piece measures 15 (16, 17, 17, 17)" from beg.

Shape armhole: BO 3 sts at beg of side edge, dec 1 st EOR 3 (4, 5, 6, 7) times as follows: K1, ssk, work in patt to end—30 (31, 32, 33, 34) sts. Cont until piece measures 20 (21, 22, 23, 23)" from beg.

Shape neck: At neck edge, BO 6 sts once, BO 3 sts once, dec 1 st EOR 3 (4, 5, 5, 5) times—18 (18, 18, 19, 20) sts.

Cont until piece measures 23 (24, 25, 26, 26)" from beg. BO all sts in patt.

left front

Work as for right front, reversing shaping. On armhole-shaping dec row, work to last 3 sts, K2tog, K1. Omit buttonholes.

sleeves

CO 28 (30, 30, 30, 32) sts, work in seed st, inc 1 st at each edge every 6 rows 11 times—50 (52, 52, 52, 54) sts. For better seams, work inc 2 sts from edge. Cont until piece measures 16½" or desired length from beg.

Shape cap: BO 3 sts at beg of next 2 rows, BO 2 sts at beg of next 2 rows, dec 1 st at each edge EOR 7 times, BO 3 sts at beg of next 4 rows—14 (16, 16, 16, 18) sts. BO rem sts in patt.

patch pockets (make 2)

CO 21 sts and work in seed st until 7" from beg. BO all sts in patt.

finishing

Sew shoulder seams.

Neckband: With RS facing you and circular needle, PU 42 (48, 54, 56, 56) sts around neck edge and work in seed st, inc 1 st at each edge every 4 rows 4 times. Cont until collar measures 5½". BO all sts in patt.

Place pockets on fronts and sew in place. Sew side and sleeve seams. Sew on buttons to match buttonhole placement. Weave in ends.

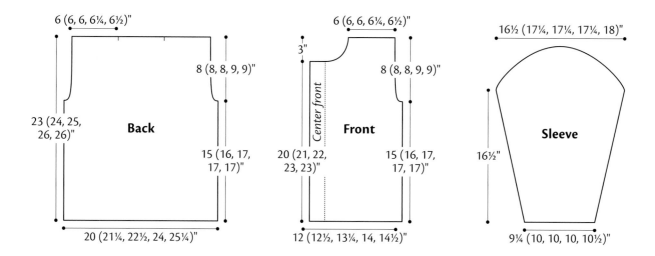

bamboo kimono

A wonderful decorative technique used by the Pueblos is incising, where grooves are drawn into clay in patterns. Here garter stitches and a change in stitch direction are used to create the elegantly simple effect.

By Kerry Ferguson

Skill Level: Intermediate ◼◼◼◻

One Size

Finished Bust Measurement: 52"

Finished Length: 27"

materials

1100 yds of bulky-weight 100% wool

Size 9 (5.5 mm) needles

Size 10½ (6.5 mm) needles or size required to obtain gauge

gauge

13 sts and 18 rows = 4" in seeded chevron st on larger needles

13 sts and 24 rows = 4" in garter st on larger needles

seeded chevron stitch

(Multiple of 22 sts + 1 st)

Row 1: K1, *P3, (K1, P1) twice, K1, P5, K1, (P1, K1) twice, P3, K1; rep from *

Row 2: P1, *P1, K3, (P1, K1) twice, P1, K3, P1, (K1, P1) twice, K3, P2; rep from *.

Row 3: K1, *K2, P3, (K1, P1) 5 times, K1, P3, K3; rep from *.

Row 4: K1, *P3, K3, (P1, K1) 4 times, P1, K3, P3, K1; rep from *.

Row 5: P1, *P1, K3, P3, (K1, P1) 3 times, K1, P3, K3, P2; rep from *.

Row 6: K1, *K2, P3, K3, (P1, K1) twice, P1, K3, P3, K3; rep from *.

Row 7: K1, *P3, K3, P3, K1, P1, K1, P3, K3, P3, K1; rep from *.

Row 8: K1, *(P1, K3, P3, K3) twice, P1, K1; rep from *.

Row 9: K1, *P1, K1, P3, K3, P5, K3, P3, K1, P1, K1; rep from *.

Row 10: K1, *P1, K1, P1, (K3, P3) twice, K3, (P1, K1) twice; rep from *.

Row 11: K1, *(P1, K1) twice, P3, K3, P1, K3, P3, (K1, P1) twice, K1; rep from *.

Row 12: K1, *(P1, K1) twice, P1, K3, P5, K3, (P1, K1) 3 times; rep from *.

Row 13: P1, *(P1, K1) 3 times, P3, K3, P3, (K1, P1) twice, K1, P2; rep from *.

Row 14: K1, *K2, (P1, K1) twice, (P1, K3) twice, (P1, K1) 3 times, K2; rep from *.

Rep rows 1–14.

body

With smaller needles, CO 133 sts. Work 17 rows in garter st.

Change to larger needles and work in seeded chevron st until piece measures 17" from beg. BO all sts.

yoke and sleeves

With larger needles, CO 12 sts for first triangle. Work in garter st, following chart for Triangle A (first row on chart is CO row). BO last 3 sts. PU 41 sts for Triangle B where shown and work in garter st, following chart for Triangle B (first row on chart is the PU row). Fasten off last st. PU 41 sts for Triangle C where shown and work in garter st, following chart for Triangle C. When all rows are complete, BO. PU 33 sts along 11" edge of Triangle C (first row of chart is pick and knit row). Work chart using short row technique as follows:

On WS rows: Knit to last 4 sts, turn work.

On following RS rows: Sl 1 st pw wyib, knit to end of row.

As you work the WS and RS rows you will be leaving 4 more unworked sts on every WS row. When you finish the last RS row of 3 sts, turn the work and BO all the sts on your needle that were left unworked on each WS row. PU 33 sts along 11" edge of Triangle C. Work 14 rows in garter st. Make 8 of these A/B/C panels.

Make 1 larger panel for the back. After 14 rows of garter st on Triangle C edge, PU 33 sts along 11" edge of Triangle A and work 14 rows in garter st.

finishing

Referring to diagrams on page 124, lay out 5 panels for back yoke and sleeves, placing larger panel at far right. Sew pieces tog. Lay out 2 panels for front yoke and sleeves for each side and sew tog. Sew sleeve and shoulder seams so that 10" gap remains in center front.

Sew underarm seams, leaving 26" open across center back and 8" across each front. Fold body piece of Kimono so that there is 26" for back and 8" for each front. Sew yoke and sleeves to body.

Front bands: With RS facing you and smaller needles, PU 88 sts along each front edge. Work 17 rows in garter st. Sew top edge to back of neck. Weave in ends.

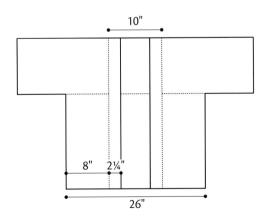

Triangle B

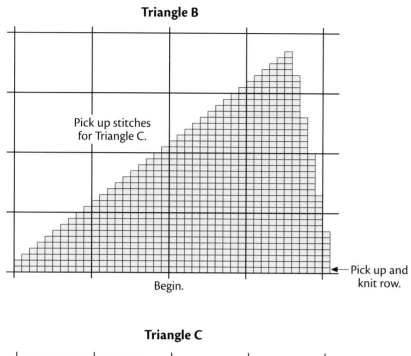

Pick up stitches
for Triangle C.

Begin.

← Pick up and
knit row.

Triangle A

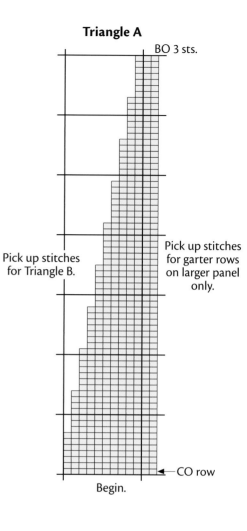

BO 3 sts.

Pick up stitches
for Triangle B.

Pick up stitches
for garter rows
on larger panel
only.

← CO row

Begin.

Triangle C

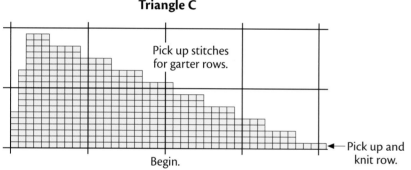

Pick up stitches
for garter rows.

Begin.

← Pick up and
knit row.

Larger panel

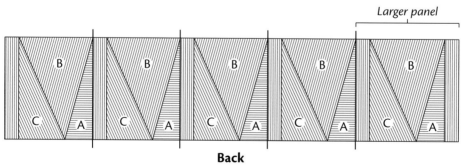

Back

Front

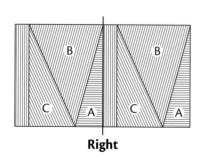

Right

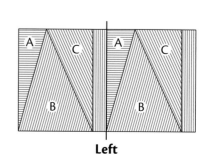

Left

abbreviations and glossary

approx   approximately

beg   begin(ning)

BO   bind off

CC   contrasting color

ch   chain

cn   cable needle

CO   cast on

cont   continue, continuing

dec(s)   decrease(s), deceasing (see also *K2tog,* and *ssk*)

dpn(s)   double-pointed needle(s)

EOR   every other row

est   established

g   grams

garter st   garter stitch; back and forth: knit every row; in the round: knit 1 round, purl 1 round

inc(s)   increase(s), increasing (see also *K1f&b* and *M1*)

K   knit

K1f&b   knit 1 stitch front and back: knit the stitch normally but do not drop the old stitch from the left needle; then knit the same stitch through the back loop and drop the old stitch—1 stitch increased

K1tbl   knit stitch through the back loop

K2tog   knit 2 together: insert the needle into 2 stitches at the same time and work them together as 1 stitch—1 stitch decreased, right slanting

LH   left hand

M1   make 1 stitch: lift horizontal strand between the needles from front to back and place on left-hand needle; knit through back loop of stitch formed (1 stitch increased)

MC   main color

oz   ounces

P   purl

P1tbl   purl stitch through the back loop

P2tog   purl 2 stitches together—1 stitch decreased

P3tog   purl 3 stitches together—2 stitches decreased

patt(s)   pattern(s)

pm   place marker

psso   pass slipped stitch(es) over

PU   pick up and knit

pw   purlwise

rem   remain(ing)

rep   repeat

rnd(s)   round(s)

RS   right side(s)

sc   single crochet

sk   skip

sl   slip

sl 1   slip 1 stitch purlwise with yarn in back unless otherwise instructed

sl 1-K2tog-psso   slip 1 stitch as if to knit, knit 2 stitches together, pass slipped stitch over—2 stitches decreased

ssk   slip, slip, knit: slip the next 2 stitches, one at a time, to the right needle as if to knit, then insert the left needle into the front of the stitches and knit the 2 stitches together as 1 stitch—1 stitch decreased, left slanting

st(s)   stitch(es)

St st   stockinette stitch; back and forth: knit RS rows and purl WS rows; in the round: knit every round

tog   together

wyib   with yarn in back

wyif   with yarn in front

WS   wrong side

yds   yards

YO(s)   yarn over(s)

techniques

Consult this section for help with the techniques used in this book.

cable cast on (cable CO)

To cast on stitches to a work that's already in progress, the cable cast-on method is a quick and easy option.

At the beginning of a row of knitting, insert the right needle between the first two stitches on the left needle, wrap the yarn around the needle as if to knit, and pull the new loop through to the front and place it on the end of the left needle to form one new stitch. Repeat for the number of stitches required.

Insert needle between two stitches. Knit a stitch.

Place new stitch on left needle.

provisional cast on

A provisional cast on is temporary, and will be removed later so that the live stitches remain intact.

1. Use a crochet hook and make a number of loose chain stitches with a contrasting slippery yarn, such as a mercerized cotton. Make one chain for each stitch of cast on needle plus a few extra.

2. Using a knitting needle, knit into the back of each chain with the yarn that will be used in the pattern. Begin knitting as instructed in the pattern.

Knit on stitches in the back of the chain.

3. To pick up the stitches, remove the crochet chain by pulling each chain out one at a time and placing the live stitches back on the knitting needle.

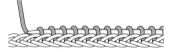

Front of chain after stitches have been picked up

backward loop cast on

This is a looser cast on that creates an edge that makes it easy to pick up stitches. Loops can be formed over the index finger or thumb and slant to the left.

THREE-NEEDLE BIND OFF

The three-needle bind off is used to join two pieces of knitting together instead of sewing a seam. Both pieces must have the same number of stitches.

1. Place the two pieces on knitting needles so the right sides of each piece are facing each other with the needles parallel.

2. Insert a third needle through the first stitch on each needle as if to knit. Knit these stitches together as one, leaving one stitch on the right-hand needle.

3. Repeat step 2 and slip the first stitch on the left-hand needle over the second stitch.

Repeat step 3 until all stitches are bound off.

crochet

Chain (ch): Wrap yarn around hook and pull through loop on hook.

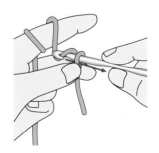

Single crochet (sc): Work from right to left with right side facing you. Insert the hook into next stitch, yarn over hook, pull loop to front, yarn over hook, and pull loop through both loops on hook. Space stitches so the edge lies flat.

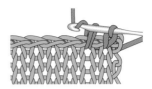

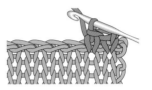

Double crochet (dc): Work from right to left with right side facing you.

1. Yarn over hook, insert hook into next stitch, yarn over hook, and pull loop to front (three loops on hook).

2. Yarn over hook and pull through first two loops on hook (two loops on hook).

3. Yarn over hook and pull through remaining two loops (one loop remains on hook).

useful information

metric conversions

Yards x .91 = meters

Meters x 1.09 = yards

Grams x .035 = ounces

Ounces x 28.35 = grams

standard yarn-weight system						
Yarn-Weight Symbol and Category Names	Super Fine **1**	Fine **2**	Light **3**	Medium **4**	Bulky **5**	Super Bulky **6**
Types of Yarns in Category	Sock, Fingering, Baby	Sport, Baby	DK, Light Worsted	Worsted, Afghan, Aran	Chunky, Craft, Rug	Bulky, Roving
Knit Gauge Ranges in Stockinette Stitch to 4"	27 to 32 sts	23 to 26 sts	21 to 24 sts	16 to 20 sts	12 to 15 sts	6 to 11 sts
Recommended Needle in U.S. Size Range	1 to 3	3 to 5	5 to 7	7 to 9	9 to 11	11 and larger
Recommended Needle in Metric Size Range	2.25 to 3.25 mm	3.25 to 3.75 mm	3.75 to 4.5 mm	4.5 to 5.5 mm	5.5 to 8 mm	8 mm and larger

skill levels

■□□□ **Beginner:** Projects for first-time knitters using basic knit and purl stitches; minimal shaping.

■■□□ **Easy:** Projects using basic stitches, repetitive stitch patterns, and simple color changes; simple shaping and finishing.

■■■□ **Intermediate:** Projects using a variety of stitches, such as basic cables and lace, simple intarsia, and techniques for double-pointed needles and knitting in the round; midlevel shaping.

■■■■ **Experienced:** Projects using advanced techniques and stitches, such as short rows, Fair Isle, more intricate intarsia, cables, lace patterns, and numerous color changes.